D0081692

The Economics of Inequality

THE ECONOMICS OF INEQUALITY

Thomas Piketty

Translated by Arthur Goldhammer

The Belknap Press of Harvard University Press

CAMBRIDGE, MASSACHUSETTS
LONDON, ENGLAND
2015

First published as *L'économie des inégalités*
copyright © Éditions La Découverte, Paris, France, 1997, 2008, 2014

First printing

Library of Congress Cataloging-in-Publication Data
Piketty, Thomas, 1971–
[L'économie des inégalités. English]
The economics of inequality / Thomas Piketty ; translated by
Arthur Goldhammer.
pages cm
Includes bibliographical references and index.
ISBN 978-0-674-50480-6 (alk. paper)
1. Income distribution. 2. Equality—Economic aspects. I. Title.
HB523.P54713   2015
339.2'2—dc23   2015008813

Book design by Dean Bornstein

Contents

Note to the Reader · vii

Introduction · 1
1. The Measurement of Inequality and Its Evolution · 5
2. Capital-Labor Inequality · 26
3. Inequality of Labor Income · 66
4. Instruments of Redistribution · 100

References · 123
Contents in Detail · 131
Index · 135

Note to the Reader

This book was written and first published in 1997. It was subsequently updated for several new editions, most recently in 2014. It should be noted, however, that the overall structure has not been changed since 1997 and that the work essentially reflects the state of knowledge and data available at that time. As a consequence, this book does not fully take into account the results of the past fifteen years of international research on the historical dynamics of inequality. In particular, recent research has demonstrated that there are important historical variations in the capital-income ratios and the capital shares in national income, and not only in the concentration of capital ownership at the individual level. That is, the macroeconomic or functional distribution of national income and national wealth is substantially less stable than what I was taught in graduate school and what I report in this book. The large historical variations in top income shares also receive insufficient treatment in the present book, because the corresponding research became fully available only recently. Readers interested in a detailed account of that more recent research and the lessons that can be drawn from it are advised to consult the World Top Incomes Database (available online) and my book *Capital in the Twenty-First Century* (Belknap Press, 2014).

The Economics of Inequality

Introduction

The question of inequality and redistribution is central to political conflict. Caricaturing only slightly, two positions have traditionally been opposed.

The right-wing free-market position is that, in the long run, market forces, individual initiative, and productivity growth are the sole determinants of the distribution of income and standard of living, in particular of the least well-off members of society; hence government efforts to redistribute wealth should be limited and should rely on instruments that interfere as little as possible with the virtuous mechanisms of the market—instruments such as Milton Friedman's negative income tax (1962).

The traditional left-wing position, passed down from nineteenth-century socialist theory and trade-union practice, holds that the only way to alleviate the misery of the poorest members of capitalist society is through social and political struggle, and that the redistributive efforts of government must penetrate to the very heart of the productive process. Opponents of the system must challenge the market forces that determine the profits of capitalists and the unequal remuneration of workers, for instance, by nationalizing the means of production or setting strict wage schedules. Merely collecting taxes to finance transfers to the poor is not enough.

This left-right conflict shows that disagreements about the concrete form and desirability of redistributive policy are not necessarily due to contradictory principles of social justice but rather to contradictory analyses of the economic and social mechanisms that produce inequality. Indeed, there exists a certain consensus in regard to the fundamental principles of social justice: if inequality is due, at least in part, to factors beyond the control of individuals, such as inequality of initial endowments owing to inheritance or luck (which cannot be attributed to individual effort), then it is just for the state to seek in the most efficient way possible to improve the lot of the least well-off (that is, of those who have had to contend with the most adverse factors). Modern theories of social justice have expressed this idea in the form of a "maximin" principle, according to which a just society ought to maximize the minimum opportunities and conditions available within the social system. The maximin principle was formally introduced by Serge-Christophe Kolm (1972) and John Rawls (1972), but one finds it more or less explicitly formulated in much earlier works—for example, in the traditional idea that everyone should be guaranteed the broadest possible range of equal rights, a concept widely accepted at the theoretical level. Often, the real conflict is about the most effective way to improve the actual standard of living of the least well-off and about the extent of the rights that can be granted to all in the name of abstract principles of social justice.

Hence only a detailed analysis of the socioeconomic mechanisms that generate inequality can sort out the competing truth claims of these two extreme versions of redistribution and perhaps contribute to the elaboration of a more just and effective set of policies. The purpose of this book is to present the current state of knowledge as a first step toward that end.

The contrast between the left- and right-wing views sketched above highlights the importance of different systems of redistribution. Should the market and its price system be allowed to operate freely, with redistribution effected solely by means of taxes and transfers, or should one attempt to alter the structure of the market forces that generate inequality? In the jargon of economics, this contrast corresponds to the distinction between *pure redistribution* and *efficient redistribution*. Pure redistribution occurs when the market equilibrium is "Pareto efficient," meaning that it is impossible to alter the allocation of resources and output in such a way that everyone gains, yet social justice nevertheless calls for redistribution from the better-off to the worse-off. Efficient redistribution occurs when the existence of market imperfections allows for direct intervention in the production process to achieve Pareto-efficient improvements in the allocation and equitable distribution of resources.

In contemporary political conflict, the distinction between pure and efficient redistribution is often conflated with the distinction between redistribution on a modest scale and redistribution on a large scale. The traditional right-left conflict has grown more complicated over time, however. For instance, some on the left advocate a "guaranteed basic income" for all citizens, to be financed by taxes without direct intervention in the market. This guaranteed basic income differs from Friedman's negative income tax solely by virtue of size. Broadly speaking, therefore, the question of how redistribution is to be achieved is separate from the question of the extent of redistribution. In this book I will try to show that it is best to treat the two questions separately, because they involve different analytical considerations and lead to different answers.

To pursue these issues further, it is useful to begin by reminding the reader of the history and extent of today's inequality. Doing so will enable us to identify the principal sets of facts that any theory of inequality and redistribution must take into account (Chapter 1). The next two chapters (2 and 3) present the leading analyses of the mechanisms that produce inequality, emphasizing both the political stakes involved in the intellectual conflict between opposing theories and the observed or observable facts that can help us decide which theories are correct. Chapter 2 looks first at inequality between capital and labor, a fundamental inequality that has deeply influenced the analysis of the social question since the nineteenth century. Chapter 3 deals with inequality of income from labor itself, which has perhaps become (if it hasn't always been) the central question in regard to contemporary inequality. It will then be possible to delve more deeply into the key issue, namely, the conditions under which redistribution becomes possible and the tools for achieving it (Chapter 4). Special attention will be paid to inequality and redistribution in France, although the relative paucity of available data and analyses (in sharp contrast to the attention devoted to unemployment, the "social fracture," and other central issues of French political debate in the 1990s) will force us at times to rely mainly on studies of other countries, especially the United States, to illustrate, confirm, or refute the theories discussed.

ONE

The Measurement of Inequality
and Its Evolution

What orders of magnitude can we associate with contemporary inequality? Is the income of the rich in a given country twice that of the poor? Ten times as great? Or a hundred times? How does the income gap in one country or period compare with that in other places at other times? Was the income gap in 1950 the same as in 1900 or 1800? Has inequality with respect to unemployment become the major form of inequality in the Western world in the 1990s?

Different Types of Income

What are the various sources of household income? Table 1.1 breaks down the income of 24 million French households in 2000 into various categories: wages, self-employment income (earned, for example, by farmers, merchants, doctors, lawyers, and so on), pensions, other transfer income (family allowances, unemployment insurance, welfare), and capital income (dividends, interest, rent, etc.).

What do we learn from Table 1.1? First, 58.8 percent of total household income comes in the form of wages. If we add to this the 5.8 percent of income consisting of self-employment compensation, we find that nearly two-thirds of total household income is compensation for labor. Social income accounts for another 30 percent of the total, and for more than two-thirds of retiree income. Finally, income from household wealth (capital income such as dividends, interest, and so on) accounts for roughly 5 percent of the total. As is well known, however, capital income is not accurately reported in household

TABLE I.I

Sources of household income in France, 2000 (percent)

	Wages	Self-employment income	Pensions	Transfers	Capital
Average	58.8	5.8	21.3	9.5	4.6
D1	17.9	1.7	43.2	34.2	3.1
D2	30.0	2.3	44.6	20.7	2.4
D3	38.3	2.9	40.8	15.1	2.9
D4	44.3	2.7	35.7	14.3	3.1
D5	50.6	2.6	28.9	14.6	3.4
D6	58.4	3.6	22.0	12.4	3.6
D7	63.3	3.4	19.8	10.4	3.2
D8	66.5	3.3	18.7	7.6	3.9
D9	68.6	4.6	16.6	5.6	4.6
P90–95	70.2	7.0	13.4	4.1	5.3
P95–100	63.6	16.4	8.4	2.9	8.8

Notes: "D1" represents the poorest 10 percent of households, "D2" the next 10 percent, and so on. "P95–100" represents the wealthiest 5 percent and "P90–95" the preceding 5 percent. Wages account on average for 58.8 percent of the total income of all households but only 17.9 percent of the income of the poorest 10 percent, 30.0 percent for the next 10 percent, and 63.6 percent for the wealthiest 5 percent.

Self-employment income includes profits from farming, industry, commerce, and other small business activities. Transfers include family allowances, unemployment insurance, and basic income. Capital income includes stock dividends, interest, and rent. All income figures are net of social charges (including the Generalized Social Contribution [CSG] and Contribution to Repayment of the Social Debt [CRDS]—see text).

Source: "2000 Family Budget Survey," INSEE (author's calculations).

income surveys. National accounts based on dividend and interest data provided by firms and banks yield a higher estimate of the share of capital income in total household income, on the order of 10 percent (INSEE, 1996b, pp. 26–29). In any case, all sources agree that labor income accounts for at least six or seven times as large a share of total household income as capital income. This is a general feature of the income distribution in all Western countries (Atkinson et al., 1995, p. 101). But the 5 to 10 percent share of household income derived from capital underestimates the share of capital income in total national income, since a substantial portion of the capital income of firms is not distributed to households (see Chapter 2).

The importance of these various types of income is obviously not the same for rich and poor. To analyze this further, it is useful to distinguish between different deciles of the income distribution: the first decile, denoted D1 in Table 1.1, includes the bottom 10 percent of the household income distribution. The second decile, D2, includes the next 10 percent, and so on, up to the top decile, D10, which represents the 10 percent of households with the highest income. To refine this description, we also use the notion of centiles: the first centile includes the bottom 1 percent of households, and so on up to the hundredth centile. Each decile includes a subgroup of the population: some 2.4 million households per decile and 240,000 per centile in the case of France in the year 2000. One can calculate various characteristics for each decile or centile: average income, for example. This should not be confused with the notion of upper income limits for each group. To capture this statistic, we use the letter P: for example, P10 represents the level of income below which we find 10 percent of all households; P90 is the upper limit below which we find 90 percent of all households; and so on. In Table 1.1, P90–95 represents the subset of all households with incomes between the top of the 90th centile and the top of the 95th centile, that is, the first half of the tenth decile, whereas P95–100 represents the second half of the tenth decile, which includes the five top-earning centiles.

Table 1.1 shows that the households in D1 consist largely of modest retirees and unemployed workers: the wages they receive account on average for 18 percent of their income, while nearly 80 percent consists of social income. The share of wages in total income increases with income level, while the share of retirees and unemployed decreases, until we reach the top 5 percent (P95–100), where capital income and nonwage compensation account for a substantial share of the total (I make no distinction between "wages" and "salary" throughout: both refer to income from labor). Nonwage compensation is intermediate in nature between labor income and capital income, since it remunerates both the labor of the farmer, doctor, or merchant and the capital invested in his or her business. Still, labor income continues to account for a very large share of the total income of households at the top of the distribution: the top 5 percent take more of their income in wages than in income from capital, no matter how the latter is estimated. One has to go even higher in the income hierarchy to reach a level where labor income no longer accounts for the largest share (Piketty, 2001).

Wage Inequality

How are wages, which represent the lion's share of household income, distributed? Table 1.2 describes wage inequality among full-time private-sector workers in France in 2000 (a group of some 12.7 million individuals).

The bottom 10 percent of the wage distribution (D1) earned on average an income roughly equal to the minimum wage, or about €890 per month (net of taxes) in 2000. The median wage (denoted P50, by definition the wage level below which lies 50 percent of the sample) was €1,400. This was higher than the average wage of the fifth decile (€1,310), since the fifth decile consists of workers between P40 and P50. It was also lower than the average wage overall, which was €1,700 in 2000, because the top half of the wage distribution is always "longer-tailed" than the bottom half, so that very high earners inevitably lift the average wage above the median. Furthermore, the best-paid 10 percent, who earn at least €2,720 per month, earn an average wage of €4,030, or nearly twice as much as the next lower 10 percent (€2,340).

One practical indicator of total wage inequality is the P90/P10 ratio, that is, the ratio of the lower limit of the tenth decile to the upper

TABLE 1.2

Wage inequality in France, 2000

Average monthly wage in euros

Average	1,700		
D1	890	900	P10
D2	1,100		
D3	1,110		
D4	1,210		
D5	1,310	1,400	P50
D6	1,450		
D7	1,620		
D8	1,860		
D9	2,340	2,720	P90
D10	4,030		

Note: D1 represents the worst-paid 10 percent; D2 the next 10 percent, and so on. P10 is the limit dividing D1 and D2, P50 the limit dividing D5 and D6, and P90 the limit dividing D9 and D10. In other words, the worst paid all earned less than €900 a month, with an average income of €890, whereas the best-paid 10 percent all earned more than €2,720, with an average income of €4,030. These figures represent monthly wages excluding bonuses net of social charges (and CSG/CRDS) for full-time, private-sector workers.

Source: DADS (Annual declaration of social data), INSEE, 2002, p. 10.

limit of the first decile. In the case of France in 2000, the P90/P10 ratio was 2,720/900 or roughly 3.0: to belong to the top-earning 10 percent, one had to make at least three times as much as the least well paid. This indicator should not be confused with the D10/D1 ratio, that is, the ratio of the average wage of the tenth decile to that of the first decile, which is by definition always higher and which in France in 2000 was 4,030/890, or 4.5: the best-paid 10 percent in France earned on average 4.5 times as much as the worst-paid 10 percent. Table 1.2 also allows us to calculate the total wages paid to the top 10 percent: since the average wage of D10 was 2.37 times the average wage (4,030/1,700 = 2.37) and the number of workers in D10 is by definition 10 percent of the total number of workers, it follows that D10 received 23.7 percent of total wages.

Other indicators are also used in order to capture the overall inequality of the distribution and not just the gap between the extreme deciles: for instance, the Gini coefficient or the Theil and Atkinson indices (Morrisson, 1996, pp. 81–96). Nevertheless, interdecile indicators (such as P90/P10, D10/D1, P80/P20, etc.) are by far the simplest and most intuitive. The P90/P10 indicator has the merit of being available in reliable numbers for many countries, hence it will be cited frequently in this chapter.

For a more complete view of wage inequality, one would need to include figures for public-sector wages in addition to private-sector wages. In France, the 4.1 million full-time employees of the public sector earn slightly more on average than private-sector workers, and public-sector wages are significantly less widely dispersed: for example, the P90/P10 ratio for civil-service workers was 2.6 (INSEE, 1996d, p. 55).

International Comparisons

Is a P90/P10 ratio of 3:1 typical of wage inequality everywhere? Table 1.3 gives the P90/P10 ratio for fourteen OECD countries in 1990.

The table shows that France, with a P90/P10 ratio of 3.1 in 1990, occupied a middle position between Germany and the Nordic countries on the one hand and the English-speaking countries on the other. In the former, the ratio was generally around 2.5, dipping as low as 2 in Norway, 2.1 in Sweden, and 2.2 in Denmark, while in the latter it was as high as 3.4 in the United Kingdom, 4.4 in Canada, and 4.5 in the United States. For all the countries shown, the figures in Table 1.3 concern only full-time employees. This is an important detail, because including part-time workers (of whom there were some 3.1 million in

TABLE 1.3

Wage inequality in OECD countries in 1990, measured by the P90/P10 ratio

Country	Ratio between best-paid and worst-paid 10 percent
Norway	2.0
Sweden	2.1
Denmark	2.2
Netherlands	2.3
Belgium	2.3
Italy	2.4
Germany	2.5
Portugal	2.7
Japan	2.8
France	3.1
United Kingdom	3.4
Austria	3.5
Canada	4.4
United States	4.5

Note: For example, in Germany the best-paid 10 percent earn at least 2.5 times as much as the worst-paid 10 percent.

Sources: OECD, 1993, pp. 170–173; US data, Katz et al., 1995, fig. 1.

France in 2000) systematically leads to larger P90/P10 ratios. For example, the OECD figures including intermittent and part-time workers in the United States in 1990 give a P90/P10 ratio of 5.5, but only 4.5 when these workers are left out (Katz et al., 1995, fig. 1; Lefranc, 1997, table 1), as is the case with other countries (OECD, 1993, p. 173). In short, P90/P10 ratios range from 2 to 4.5, which is considerable variation for countries at very similar levels of economic development.

Income Inequality

How does this inequality between workers translate into inequality of household income? The answer is not simple, because one has to add nonwage compensation of the self-employed (some 3 million individuals in France in 2000), social transfers, and capital income, and then individual wage earners, non–wage earners, and their children have to be grouped together to form households. Table 1.4 presents the results for France in 2000.

The average monthly household income in France was €2,280, but 10 percent of households had less than €790 of monthly income,

TABLE 1.4

Income inequality in France, 2000

Monthly income in euros

Average	2,280		
D1	540	790	P10
D2	930	1,070	P20
D3	1,190	1,330	P30
D4	1,480	1,610	P40
D5	1,760	1,920	P50
D6	2,080	2,240	P60
D7	2,430	2,630	P70
D8	2,880	3,150	P80
D9	3,570	4,090	P90
P90–95	4,520	5,100	P95
P95–100	7,270		

Notes: See Tables 1.1 and 1.2. The poorest 10 percent of households have income of less than €790 per month, averaging €540. The wealthiest 5 percent have income above €5,100 per month, with an average of €7,300. Monthly income calculated by dividing annual income by twelve, including wages, self-employment income, pensions, transfers, and capital income. Income is net of social charges (including CSG/CRDS) but not of other direct taxes (income tax, housing tax).
Source: "2000 family budget survey," INSEE (author's calculations).

while 10 percent had more than €4,090, for a P90/P10 ratio for total household income of 5.2 (compare with the P90/P10 ratio for wages of 3.0). The top 5 percent of households, with monthly income above €5,100, had an average monthly income of €7,270.

The fact that inequality of household income is greater than wage inequality is quite common, and it was made worse in France in 2000 by the fact that many households included unemployed workers. In general, however, the explanation of this difference depends on factors other than unemployment.

First, nonwage income and especially capital income are much more unequally distributed than wages. Typically, the share of capital income claimed by the wealthiest 10 percent of households is on the order of 50 percent of total capital income, as is the share of total wealth owned by the wealthiest 10 percent, whereas the share of total wages going to the highest-paid 10 percent falls between 20 and 30 percent (23.7 percent in France in 2000). The share of capital income in total income is low, however, so the share of income going to the wealthiest 10 percent of households was just 26 percent of total household income in France in 2000. These very large disparities of wealth, much greater than wage and income inequalities, are also much less well known. Inequalities of wealth cannot be explained solely by inequalities of present and past income. Behavioral differences with respect to savings and accumulation also play a part (accounting for nearly half of wealth inequality in 1992, according to Lollivier and Verger [1996]). These specific difficulties of accounting for wealth inequality explain why measures of inequality are often limited to inequalities of wages and income.

But the main reason why income inequality is always significantly greater than wage inequality is totally different: it comes from the fact that a majority of low-income households are households living on small pensions, often consisting of one person, whereas high-income households are generally couples, often with two earners and children living at home. If one were to calculate the P90/P10 ratio not for household income but for household income adjusted for household size in order to measure inequality in standards of living rather than of income as such, one would find a ratio of 4.3–4.4 rather than 5.2, depending on how the adjustment was made (INSEE, 1996b, p. 16). If one is interested in disposable income, then the effect of taxes on income also needs to be taken into account, which the figures in Table 1.4 do not do. This would reduce the P90/P10 ratio by about 10 percent, since the income tax paid by a household with income at the P90 level, about €4,090 per month, would average about 10 percent, while households at the P10 level pay no income tax (INSEE, 1995, p. 19). (On the redistributive effect of taxes and transfers, see Chapter 4.) We would thus arrive at a ratio for disposable household income adjusted for household size of 3.5–4, slightly greater than wage inequality.

International Comparisons

How does a P90/P10 ratio of 3.5–4 compare with what we see in other countries? International comparisons are unfortunately much more difficult to do for household incomes than for wages: it is often difficult to include exactly the same income categories in all countries. Culminating an ambitious effort to compile comparable data for many countries, the Luxembourg Income Study (LIS) was published in 1995 at the behest of the OECD (Atkinson et al., 1995).

The P90/P10 ratios in Table 1.5 are for disposable income, that is, income accounting for taxes and transfers, and adjusted for household size. France is assigned a ratio of 3.5 (and not 5.2 as in Table 1.4) for that reason, along with the fact that the OECD study used 1984 fiscal data rather than the "Family Budget Survey" of 2000. The same international contrast observed earlier in relation to wage inequalities occurs again here: Germany, Belgium, Sweden, and Norway, which had wage ratios of 2–2.5, have income ratios of 2.7–3, while the United Kingdom, United States, and Canada, which had wage ratios of 3.5–4.5,

TABLE 1.5

Income inequality in OECD countries

Country	P90/P10 ratio
Sweden	2.7
Belgium	2.8
Norway	2.9
Germany	3.0
France	3.5
United Kingdom	3.8
Italy	4.0
Canada	4.0
United States	5.9

Notes: In Sweden, to belong to the top 10 percent in income, one must earn at least 2.7 times as much as anyone in the bottom 10 percent. The table shows the P90/P10 ratio for disposable income adjusted for household size (Atkinson et al., 1995). Years: 1984 (Germany, France), 1985 (Australia), 1986 (US, Italy, Norway, UK), 1987 (Canada, Sweden), 1988 (Belgium).

Source: LIS, Atkinson, Rainwater, and Smeeding, 1995, p. 40.

have income ratios of 3.8–5.9, with the United States topping the chart at 5.9. France again occupies an intermediate position.

It is extremely difficult to compare these figures with the few available inequality indicators from outside the developed world. Conditions vary widely: the South American countries stand out for having even higher levels of inequality than the most inegalitarian Western countries, whereas most Asian countries, as well as the less-developed countries of Africa, generally have levels of income inequality equal to or less than those found in the least inegalitarian Western countries (Morrisson, 1996, pp. 145–172). It is also difficult to compare levels of inequality found in the Communist bloc, because income often includes compensation in kind in one form or another and is difficult to quantify in monetary terms. The available indicators seem to show real income gaps quite comparable to the average in capitalist countries and generally greater than in the more egalitarian capitalist countries (Morrisson, 1996, p. 140).

Inequalities in Time and Space

Are P90/P10 wage and income ratios of 3:1 or 4:1 between people living in one country at one point in time negligible compared with the gap between a citizen of an advanced country in 1990 and of the same country in 1900 or a citizen of India in 1990? Table 1.6 indicates the average purchasing power of a French blue-collar worker and of an executive from 1870 to 1994 measured in 1994 francs (that is, accounting for changes in the cost of living).

These figures should obviously be viewed cautiously: the further back we go in time, the more problematic the idea of a synthetic cost index becomes, because modes of consumption change so much. Still, orders of magnitude may be taken as significant: between 1870 and 1994, the purchasing power of a worker increased roughly

TABLE 1.6

Inequality in France from 1870–1994

Year	Blue-collar workers	White-collar workers	Middle managers	Executives
1870	960			4,360
1910	1,760			6,820
1950	2,200	2,615	3,740	7,330
1994	7,250	7,180	10,740	20,820

Note: Purchasing power in 1994 francs of average net monthly wages of different categories of workers.

Sources: For 1950 and 1994, DADS, INSEE, 1996a, pp. 44, 56. For blue-collar workers in 1870 and 1910, Lhomme, 1968, p. 46. The 1910–1950 comparison is based on Kuczynski's series for wages and General Statistics of France (SGF) for prices (INSEE, 1994, pp. 142, 152). Wage ratios of executives and workers of 3.9 in 1910 and 4.6 in 1870 were calculated on the basis of ratios between laborers, skilled workers, and executives in Morrisson, 1991, p. 154.

eightfold. This spectacular increase in standard of living during the last century of capitalism was more or less comparable in all the Western countries. For example, the hourly wage of an American worker increased by a factor of eleven between 1870 and 1990, for an average rate of increase of about 2 percent per year (Duménil and Lévy, 1996, chap. 15), which is approximately the same as in France if we take the decrease in annual hours of work into account.

This 10:1 ratio between 1990 and 1870 is approximately equivalent to, or slightly less than, the ratio of the average income of a Western citizen in 1990 to that of a Chinese or Indian citizen, using the best available estimates of purchasing power parity (Drèze and Sen, 1995, p. 213). The gaps in GDP per capita, which are often four to five times greater, don't actually make much sense, because they are expressed in terms of official exchange rates with the advanced economies, and these rates are a very poor gauge of actual differences in purchasing power. A 10:1 gap between the average standard of living in the wealthiest countries and that in the poorest countries probably comes closer to reality.

To sum up, inequality between the top 10 percent and bottom 10 percent in a given country, as measured by the P90/P10 ratio, is on the order of 3–4, and this is two to three times smaller than the gap in standard of living between the end of the nineteenth century and the end of the twentieth century and than the gap between the richest and poorest countries. These two forms of inequality are therefore not incomparable, even if one is undeniably larger than the other.

The Historical Evolution of Inequality

Are these 3:1 ratios between top and bottom income groups in one country and 10:1 ratios between rich and poor countries destined to remain steady, increase, or decrease?

Although Marx and other nineteenth-century social theorists did not quantify inequality this way, they were certain of the answer: the

logic of the capitalist system was to increase inequality between social classes—between capitalists and proletarians—constantly. The
gap between rich and poor countries would also grow. These predictions were soon challenged, however, even within the socialist camp.
In the 1890s Eduard Bernstein insisted that Marx's proletarianization
thesis did not hold because the social structure was clearly becoming
more diverse and wealth was spreading to ever broader segments of
society.

It was not until after World War II, however, that it became possible to measure the decrease in wage and income inequality in the
Western countries. New predictions were soon forthcoming. The most
celebrated was that of Simon Kuznets (1955): according to Kuznets,
inequality would everywhere be described by an inverted U curve. In
the first phase of development, inequality would increase as traditional
agricultural societies industrialized and urbanized. This would be
followed by a second phase of stabilization, and then a third phase
in which inequality would substantially decrease. This pattern—of
growing inequality in the nineteenth century followed by declining
inequality after that, has been well studied in the case of the United
Kingdom (Williamson, 1985) and the United States (Williamson and
Lindert, 1980). In the latter, for example, one finds that the share of
total wealth owned by the wealthiest 10 percent rose from 50 percent
in 1770 to a maximum of 70–80 percent in the late nineteenth century, before declining to about 50 percent, a level typical of contemporary wealth inequality. The available sources suggest that the pattern
was similar in all the Western countries.

The most recent research on France and the United States (Piketty,
2001; Piketty and Saez, 2003; Landais, 2007) shows, however, that the
sharp decrease in inequality observed over the course of the twentieth
century is in no sense the consequence of a "natural" economic process. Only inequality of wealth decreased (the wage hierarchy showing
no tendency toward compression over the long run), and this decrease
was due mainly to shocks incurred by wealth owners in the period

FIGURE 1.1. The fall of rentiers and the stability of the wage hierarchy in France, 1913–2005. Sources: Piketty, 2001; Landais, 2007.

1914–1945 (wars, inflation, the Great Depression). The concentration of wealth and capital income did not return to the astronomical level achieved on the eve of World War I, however. The most likely explanation involves the fiscal revolution of the twentieth century. The impact of the progressive income tax (created in France in 1914) and the progressive estate tax (created in 1901) on the accumulation and reconstitution of large fortunes seems to have prevented a return to nineteenth-century rentier society. If contemporary societies have become societies of managers—that is, societies in which the top of the income distribution is dominated by the "working rich" (people who live mainly on their labor income rather than on income derived from capital accumulated in the past), it is primarily a consequence of particular historical circumstances and institutions. The Kuznets curve is thus not the "end of history" but the product of a specific—and reversible—historical process.

From Laws of History to Uncertainties

The fatal blow to the Kuznets curve—the idea of an inverted U-shaped curve linking development inexorably to increasing and then decreasing inequality—came in the 1980s, when inequality began to increase in the advanced economies. This inversion of the Kuznets curve spelled an end to the notion that there was a grand historical law governing the evolution of inequality, at least for a time. It also encouraged extensive and detailed research into the complex mechanisms that might explain why inequality increases in some periods and decreases in others.

Table 1.7 describes the evolution of wage inequality in the Western economies since 1970. Inequality actually increased only in the United States and United Kingdom, but wage inequality ceased to decrease everywhere in the 1980s. This set the Western countries apart from less developed countries, where no such tendency has been detected (Davis, 1992). In the United States, the P90/P10 ratio for wages increased by about 20 percent between 1980 and 1990, for a total increase of nearly 50 percent over the entire period, which is considerable in view of the habitually slow rate of change of wage inequality. The result was that wage inequality in the United States returned to levels last seen between the two world wars (Goldin and Margo, 1992). As a logical consequence of this evolution, wealth inequality, which had been decreasing until 1970, seems to have begun to rise again (Wolff, 1992).

The case of the United Kingdom was very different, because wage inequality there was quite low in 1970, very close to Scandinavian levels. After increasing slightly in the second half of the 1970s, the P90/P10 ratio jumped nearly 30 percent between 1980 and 1990, and in the 1990s the United Kingdom joined the United States at the head

TABLE 1.7

The growth of wage inequality since 1970, as measured by the P90/P10 ratio

Country	1970	1980	1990
Germany	–	2.5	3.5
United States	3.2	3.8	4.5
France	3.7	3.2	3.2
Italy	–	2.3	2.5
Japan	–	2.5	2.8
United Kingdom	2.5	2.6	3.3
Sweden	2.1	2.0	2.1

Note: To belong to the best-paid 10 percent in the United States, one had to earn at least 3.2 times as much as anyone in the worst-paid 10 percent in 1970, compared with 4.5 times as much in 1990.

Sources: Germany, Italy, Japan, Sweden: OECD, 1993, pp. 170–173. France: INSEE, 1996a, p. 48. United States, United Kingdom: Katz et al., 1995, fig. 1.

of the pack in inequality. In the Nordic countries, inequality held steady, with P90/P10 ratios on the order of 2–2.5, despite a slight upward trend. France was a somewhat special case, since French wage inequality was the highest in the Western world in 1970 before decreasing rapidly in the 1970s and then stabilizing between 1980 and 1990, with a very slight increase since 1983–1984: the P90/P10 ratio was 3.1 in 1984, then rose to 3.2 in the period 1984–1995 (INSEE, 1996a, p. 48). Hence it was only in the 1970s that the wage distribution in the United States became more unequal than in France, while the United Kingdom did not surpass France until the late 1980s, and then by just a hair (Table 1.7). Although wage inequality in Italy was significantly lower than in France initially, its evolution in the period 1970–2000 resembled that of France: after decreasing rapidly in the 1970s and early 1980s, the P90/P10 ratio began to climb again in 1984 (Erickson and Ichino, 1995).

From Wages to Incomes

The evolution of income inequality has not been measured as well as that of wage inequality. Nevertheless, the Luxembourg Income Study data do allow us to describe in broad outline the evolution of the P90/P10 ratio for disposable household income adjusted for household size (Atkinson et al., 1995, p. 47). The countries in which wage inequality increased also saw increases in income inequality: in the United States, for example, the P90/P10 ratio for income rose from 4.9 to 5.9 between 1979 and 1986, and in the United Kingdom from 3.5 to 3.8. Conversely, inequality increased moderately in the Nordic countries, rising from 2.8 to 2.9 in Norway and 2.5 to 2.7 in Sweden, following the similarly modest increase in wage inequality. In France, the P90/P10 ratio has remained stable at 3.5 since the early 1980s after a sharp decrease in the 1970s. Since the early 1990s, there has been a slight upward trend in the P90/P10 ratio in France, although the increase was just barely statistically significant (INSEE, 1996b, pp. 36–37). In all Western countries, it is clear that the downward trend of the previous period has been reversed: income inequality, like wage inequality, ceased to decrease everywhere in the 1980s and 1990s, and it increased significantly in those countries where wage inequality resumed its upward trend. The Kuznets curve is definitely dead.

It would be a mistake, however, to interpret the evolution of income inequality as a simple mechanical consequence of the evolution of wage inequality, even though the latter is undeniably the main force at work (Gottschalk, 1993). For example, nearly half of the increase in US household income inequality between 1970 and 1990 was in fact due to increased correlation of the incomes of members of the same household: in other words, high earners are increasingly likely to marry other high earners, whereas the lowest earners are often single women with children (Meyer, 1995). Furthermore, taxes and transfers have evolved in different ways in different Western countries since the 1970s: whereas the United States and United Kingdom adopted policies that tended to increase income inequality, other countries adopted policies that sought to limit it. It is striking to compare the United States and Canada: although the labor market and wage inequality evolved in similar ways in both countries, the P90/P10 ratio for household income held steady at around 4 in Canada but rose from 4.9 to 5.9 in the United States (Atkinson et al., 1995, p. 47). The reasons for this are complex, but different fiscal and social policies explain a great deal (Card and Freeman, 1993).

Inequality with Respect to Employment

More broadly, it would be misleading to suggest that the evolution of inequality in a country like France since the 1970s can be summed up by saying that the P90/P10 wage ratio has remained more or less constant. And while many countries, including France, have kept the P90/P10 ratio for disposable household income relatively constant, this has been possible only because social transfers have been able to compensate for the loss of income owing to the growing number of the unemployed. Without transfers (including unemployment insurance, basic income support, etc.), income inequality would have increased as much as in the English-speaking countries, despite the stability of the wage income distribution: labor income inequality among all individuals of working age (and not just the employed) increased considerably in France after 1980, at a rate comparable to that observed in the English-speaking countries (Bourguignon and Martinez, 1996). Actual inequality of income from labor (whether due to employment inequality or wage inequality) has thus increased in all Western countries since the 1970s.

Is it really possible to draw a clear distinction between the English-speaking countries, where rising income inequality is supposedly a matter of increasing wage inequality, and other countries, where it is supposedly a matter of unequal risk of unemployment? Official figures might seem to support this view: the 1996 unemployment rate was

5.6 percent in the United States and 7.5 percent (and rapidly declining) in the United Kingdom, compared with 10.3 percent in Germany, 12.1 percent in Italy, and 12.2 percent in France (where 3 million people were unemployed in a working-age population of around 25 million [OECD, 1996, A24]). High growth in the late 1990s significantly reduced unemployment everywhere but left the geographical variation intact: in 2000, the unemployment rate was 4 percent in the United States and 10 percent in France (OECD, 2000).

The problem with this type of comparison, however, is that the notion of *unemployment* is not an adequate measure of the phenomenon of *underemployment*. In the United States, for example, there has been a substantial withdrawal of less-skilled individuals from the labor market (and from the group of people classified in official statistics as "actively seeking work") since the 1970s. This is entirely due to the collapse of low-wage employment opportunities (Juhn et al., 1991; Topel, 1993). Many people of working age have thus found themselves excluded from the labor market, yet they are not counted in unemployment statistics. One striking manifestation of this can be seen in the impressive increase of the prison population. In 1995, 1.5 million individuals were incarcerated in US prisons, compared with 500,000 in 1980; it is estimated that 2.4 million will be incarcerated in 2000 (Freeman, 1996). This aspect of underemployment, entirely neglected in official unemployment statistics, is not a minor matter, since these 1.5 million prisoners represented 1.5 percent of the US working age population in 1995. In France, by comparison, the prison population was just 60,000, or 0.3 percent of the working age population. It would of course be simplistic to suggest that the growth of crime in the United States since 1970 can be explained entirely by the evolution of wage inequality. Clearly, however, it was more difficult to be a model proletarian in the United States in 1995 than it was in 1970, given that the wage of the tenth centile fell by nearly 50 percent compared with that of the ninetieth centile.

It is therefore tempting to conclude that underemployment is in fact as high in the United States as in the European countries where unemployment is high. This is misleading, however, since the phenomenon of hidden underemployment is unfortunately not limited to the United States. It takes other forms in Europe, less visible perhaps but no less significant. Consider, for example, the fact that only 67 percent of the working age population is classified as belonging to the active population in France in 1996, compared with 77 percent in the United States, 75 percent in the United Kingdom, and only 68 percent in Germany and 60 percent in Italy (OECD, 1996, A22). This indicator, known as the labor market participation rate, is highly imperfect because it mixes together a wide range of phenomena, such as the female participation rate and the percentage of early retirees, but it nevertheless points to a real problem. For example, it is well known that, in France, in order to decrease the number of unemployed by one, more than one job must be created, indeed something close to two jobs, since some fraction of newly created jobs will in fact be taken by people who were not counted as part of the active population but who were prepared to enter the labor market if an appropriate job presented itself. In addition, involuntary part-time work (by people working part-time who claim to want to work more) has been increasing rapidly in France (CSERC, 1996, p. 50). Uncertainties such as these reveal the limits of our ability to correctly measure inequality with respect to employment, which is a fundamental feature of contemporary inequality.

{ TWO }

Capital-Labor Inequality

Since the industrial revolution, and in particular since the work of Karl Marx (1818–1883), the question of social inequality and redistribution has been posed primarily in terms of the opposition between capital and labor, profits and wages, employers and employees. Inequality is thus described as a contrast between those who own capital, that is, the means of production, and those who do not and must therefore make do with what they can earn from their labor. The fundamental source of inequality is thus said to be the unequal ownership of capital. Initially, the two terms of this basic inequality, capitalists and workers, are conceived as homogeneous groups, and inequality of income from labor is regarded as a secondary matter. This view of inequality as purely a question of capital versus labor has exerted, and will continue to exert, a profound influence on the way redistribution is conceptualized, even in countries that have not gone so far as to abolish private ownership of capital.

The special attention accorded to labor-capital inequality should come as no surprise. Indeed, the mere fact that a share of productive income goes to capital might seem to contradict basic principles of justice and immediately raise the question of redistribution: Why should a person who inherits ownership of capital receive income denied to those who inherit only their labor power? Absent any market inefficiency, this would amply justify a pure redistribution of capital income to labor income (using the distinction between pure and efficient redistribution discussed in the Introduction). How large should this pure redistribution be, and with what tools might it be accomplished? What does the history of this kind of redistribution and of the capital-labor split tell us?

Social justice is not the only reason to worry about the capital-labor split, however. Is the unequal distribution of wealth among individuals and countries not only unjust but also *inefficient,* because it reproduces itself by limiting the ability of the poor to invest and thus close the gap between themselves and the rich? If so, how can capital be efficiently redistributed?

The Share of Capital in Total Income

The question seems simple. A nation produces what it produces using a certain quantity of capital (machinery, infrastructure, etc.) and a certain quantity of labor (hours worked). What determines the share of output going, respectively, to capital (in the form of dividends and interest paid to the owners of capital) and labor (in the form of wages paid to workers), and what can government do to redistribute these shares? This question, and especially the role of the price system in determining the capital-labor split, has given rise to unusually acrimonious intellectual and political controversy, especially among economists.

The Question of Capital/Labor Substitution

Suppose, to begin with, that the technology that allows the nation to produce from available quantities of capital and labor is characterized by what economists call fixed coefficients: in order to produce 1 unit of output, exactly 1 unit of capital and n units of labor are required. In other words, in order to operate a particular machine properly, exactly n workers are required, neither more nor less.

When posed in these terms, the distribution of income between capital and labor is a purely distributive question; efficiency does not come into it. The only decision to be made is how to divide the 1 unit produced between the two factors of production, capital and labor. Or, to put it another way, between the owner of the machine and the n

27

workers, independent of the production process itself. Market forces and the price system play no part in determining the allocation of resources at the macroeconomic level, because no matter what price firms pay for each unit of capital and labor, they must employ n workers and 1 machine to produce 1 unit of output. In particular, the level of employment is fixed: it is entirely determined by the capital stock, that is, by the productive capacity of the economy. Without any governmental redistribution, the capital-labor split will depend on the negotiating power of unions and the ability of the employer to appropriate a portion of the product: in short, on the relative power of capitalists and workers. The key fact here is that the prices paid for capital and labor will have no effect on the level of production or the volume of employment. The capital-labor split is the outcome of a pure distributional conflict.

Under these conditions, there is no reason to ask how capital/labor redistribution is carried out: the question of redistributive instruments does not arise. Income might be redistributed to labor by increasing the wage paid to each worker: for example, by raising the minimum wage or supporting union demands for higher wages. Or the same thing might be accomplished by raising taxes on capital to finance a fiscal transfer to each worker (or to reduce the taxes paid by workers). *Direct redistribution* from profits to wages is completely equivalent to *fiscal redistribution* (via taxes and transfers); in either case there is no interference with the so-called *primary distribution,* which is determined by firms, because the total quantities of capital and labor employed in production are fixed.

Of course, it may be desirable to give the owners of capital incentives to invest and accumulate more capital in order to increase the economy's future productive capacity, and this may limit the desirable degree of redistribution from capital to labor. But this objection (whose practical implications we will examine later) applies to any attempt to decrease capital's share of total income, regardless of whether redistribution is achieved directly or indirectly (by taxes and transfers). Since the capital-labor split is a purely distributive matter, how it is achieved is of no importance; only the result matters.

What Capital/Labor Substitution Means

Different conclusions would follow if it were possible to vary the proportions of capital and labor in the production process. Suppose that 1 unit of capital no longer requires exactly n units of labor and that we can increase output by adding labor, because some tasks done by machines can also be done by workers. More generally, even if a given firm with a given production technology cannot efficiently use more than n workers per machine, it might still be possible for other firms in other sectors of the economy to use less capital-intensive and more labor-intensive technologies. For example, the service sector, which generally uses more labor and less capital than industry, might grow larger, so that for a given stock of capital, the economy as a whole would employ more workers. Thus the possibility of substituting labor for capital or vice versa is not simply a matter of technological opportunity but also a consequence of structural transformation of a society's modes of production and consumption.

If capital can be substituted for labor and vice versa, then (in contrast to the case of fixed-coefficient technology) the prices of capital and labor can play an important role in determining the quantities of each of the two factors of production used at the macroeconomic level. In a market economy, firms will hire more workers as long as doing so brings in more money than it costs, hence as long as the marginal productivity of labor, which is defined as the additional output obtained by using one additional unit of labor with the same quantity of capital, is greater than the price of labor, which is determined by the costs (in wages, social charges, bonuses, and so on) the firm incurs for employing an additional worker.

The same is true for capital, with the price of capital measured by the costs (interest and dividends, depreciation, maintenance, etc.) the firm incurs for using one additional unit of capital. Labor-intensive firms will grow more rapidly than capital-intensive firms if the price of labor is low compared with the price of capital, because consumer demand for labor-intensive goods will increase if their price is low (and conversely). In other words, the quantities of labor and capital used in a market economy, and therefore the levels of output and employment, will depend on the prices of capital and labor: prices play an *allocative* and not just a *distributive* role.

The concept of the capital-labor split and of the role played by the price system, centered on the idea of permanent adjustment of the amount of capital and labor used by firms as a function of the prices they face, was explicitly introduced by the so-called marginalist economists in the 1870s. Their notion of the marginal productivity of the factors of production broke with the thinking of classical economists such as David Ricardo and Karl Marx, who implicitly reasoned in terms of fixed-coefficient technology, so that the available capital stock entirely determined the economy's productive capacity and level of employment, thus making the capital-labor split a pure distributive conflict. The opposition between the classical and marginalist theories of the capital-labor split resurfaced in the 1950s and 1960s in the so-called "Cambridge capital controversy," which pitted economists in Cambridge, England, who insisted that the split was in essence a purely distributive conflict and emphasized the role of bargaining power, against other economists in Cambridge, Massachusetts, who argued that the relative prices of capital and labor also played an allocative role, drawing on Robert Solow's idea of the aggregate production function, a mathematical representation of the possibility of capital-labor substitution at the level of the economy as a whole.

Redistribution: "Fiscal" or "Direct"?

What are the implications of capital-labor substitutability for redistribution? If one tries to redistribute capital income to labor by increasing workers' wages, thereby increasing the price of labor, firms (and therefore the economy as a whole) will use less labor and more capital, so that the level of employment will decrease, and labor's share of total income will increase less than the initial wage increase might have led one to believe. This would not happen with fiscal redistribution (as described earlier): if one taxed the profits of firms (or capital income paid by firms to capital-owning households), one could finance a fiscal transfer or tax decrease to achieve the same redistribution of income to workers without increasing the labor costs of firms and thus without triggering a substitution of capital for labor deleterious to employment.

The essential difference between these two types of redistribution is that the contribution of firms is not calculated in the same way: direct redistribution requires firms to contribute to redistribution in proportion to the number of workers they employ, whereas fiscal redistribution requires firms to contribute only in proportion to their profits, no matter how much capital or labor they employ to produce those profits. Fiscal redistribution thus makes it possible to separate the price the firm pays for labor from the price that workers charge for their services and thus to preserve the allocative role of the price system while still redistributing income. By contrast, with direct redistribution, these two prices are necessarily equal, so that redistribution inevitably has undesirable allocative consequences.

The foregoing argument shows why it is important to distinguish between the means of redistribution and the amount. Regardless of the amount of redistribution desired, fiscal redistribution is preferable to direct redistribution in a market economy where capital-labor substitution is possible. The argument also shows that redistributions are not all alike: some are more efficient than others, in the sense that they allow the same degree of improvement in the standard of living of workers without decreasing the level of employment. The key point is that one cannot judge the effects of any form of redistribution simply by looking at who pays: it is essential to consider the effects of the proposed redistribution on the economic system as a whole.

Furthermore, redistributions based on taxes and transfers are not all alike: it is not enough to look at who pays any given tax to judge the actual consequences of a particular form of redistribution. The "fiscal incidence" of the tax matters. For example, increasing the social charges paid by firms for each employed worker is tantamount to increasing the price of labor, unless firms lower their wages to compensate for the increased charges, thereby negating the redistributive effect. By contrast, increasing taxes on corporate profits (retained or distributed) does not increase the price of labor to the firm and thus makes it possible to finance the same social transfer payments in a more efficient way than by increasing social charges. Taxes paid by firms do not all have the same effects in terms of effective redistribution: if the ultimate incidence of a tax is truly to fall on capital, its amount must depend on the level of capital used or on the income to capital.

This argument also illustrates a key result of modern economic theory: in pure (as opposed to efficient) redistribution, where redistribution is justified by considerations of pure social justice rather than by any supposed market failure, redistribution should be achieved by means of taxes and transfers rather than by manipulation of the price system. This is a very general idea: for example, it is more efficient to help the poor cope with high prices by means of fiscal transfers than by establishing price controls, because price controls lead to shortages and rationing. We will encounter this idea again when we analyze inequality and redistribution of labor income in Chapter 3.

The Elasticity of Substitution between Capital and Labor

In the special case of redistribution between capital and labor, the implications of the finding that fiscal redistribution is preferable to direct redistribution depend, however, on the degree of capital/labor substitutability and therefore on the importance of the allocative role played by the price system. No one would argue that capital-labor substitution is completely impossible. In order to determine whether fiscal redistribution is truly superior to direct redistribution, we must ask two questions: How much variation is possible in the amounts of capital and labor used at the macroeconomic level? And what influence do the prices of capital and labor have on the amounts of each the economy uses? If capital/labor substitutability is low, direct distribution has the advantage of being simple and transparent: why let the market determine the income flowing to capital and labor and establish a complex system of taxes and transfers to redistribute that income if a comparable result can be obtained by directly requiring firms to divide revenues between capital and labor in a manner deemed to be just?

To measure the degree of capital/labor substitutability and the allocative role of the price system, economists rely on the notion of *elasticity of substitution between capital and labor*. This is defined as the percentage reduction in the quantity of capital used by firms when the price of capital increases by 1 percent relative to the price of labor. This elasticity measures not only the choices of individual firms (to lay off workers, say, if the price of labor increases and to hire additional workers if it decreases) but, more importantly, the macroeconomic consequences of these individual firm-level decisions (for example, a labor-intensive sector may hire new workers less rapidly and grow more slowly if the price of labor rises and hire more rapidly and grow faster if the price of labor falls).

A high elasticity indicates that it is easy, if need be, for the economy as a whole to replace capital by labor, and vice versa: in this case, one says that there is a high elasticity of substitution between capital and labor. If the elasticity of substitution is greater than 1, a 1 percent increase in wages reduces the quantity of labor used by more than 1 percent, so that labor's share of income decreases. An elasticity equal to 1 percent corresponds to the case in which the two effects exactly balance each other, so that labor's share of income is constant, regardless of the price of labor and capital. This corresponds to the case of a Cobb-Douglas production function, named for the two economists who developed it in the 1920s after observing the division of income between profits and wages in American and Australian industry, from which they concluded that the function they found correctly accounted for what they observed (see Douglas, 1976, for a posthumous overview). We will see later whether their analysis is consistent with more recent data and studies. Conversely, an elasticity of substitution of less than 1 brings us closer to the case of fixed-coefficient technology: in this case, the marginal productivity of capital and labor falls off rapidly as one departs from the norm of n workers per machine, hence capital's share of income decreases and labor's share of income increases when the price of labor rises. The extreme case of completely fixed coefficients corresponds to zero elasticity of substitution: no deviation from the norm of n workers per machine is possible. The capital-labor split then becomes a purely distributive problem, and we are faced with the distributive conflict described by classical theory, as discussed earlier.

The debates stirred by high unemployment in Europe in the 1980s and 1990s illustrate the political issues raised by the question of elasticity of substitution between capital and labor. Many commentators suggested that the considerable increase of taxes on labor (especially in the form of social contributions) and the decrease of taxes on capital (lower taxes on profits and tax exemptions granted to the income from many forms of capital owned by households) contributed to the increase in unemployment in Europe after 1970 by increasing the cost of labor and thus encouraging firms to use more capital and less labor, or at least by reducing their incentive to use more labor and penalizing the development of labor-intensive sectors. This led to proposals to shift some of the burden on labor to capital, for example, by requiring firms to pay social contributions not on their total wage bill but on their profits, or by broadening the base of social contributions from wages to capital income (in France, the Generalized Social Contribution, or CSG, is an example of this). The practical value of such proposals depends entirely on the quantitative magnitude of the elasticity of substitution between capital and labor. If this elasticity is high, then such measures can indeed finance social spending while creating additional jobs, thus leading to more efficient redistribution. But if this elasticity is low, then such tax reform measures are illusory. And if one really wants to make capital pay more, then why not increase wages, which would not decrease the level of employment because that level is fixed, instead of inventing new taxes to replace social contributions?

The Elasticity of Capital Supply

The elasticity of substitution between capital and labor is therefore the crucial parameter for deciding what instruments of redistribution are most effective, but it does not answer the question of the desirable extent of redistribution from the workers' point of view. In fact, when considering the optimal level of redistribution, whether by direct or fiscal means, one needs to consider the effect of redistribution on the future stock of capital in the economy. A decrease in capital's share of income, whether due to higher taxes on capital or increased wages, may decrease the ability of firms to finance new investment and reduce the incentives of households to save and invest their savings in firms.

How important in practice are these negative effects of redistribution on saving and capital accumulation? The extreme traditional position is that they are so important that it is in the interest of workers not to reduce the income of capital, because any redistribution of income from capital to labor will always decrease the capital stock so much that the productivity of labor, and therefore wages, will also decrease, even if wages are supplemented by fiscal transfers (Judd, 1985; Lucas, 1990b). In that case, a pragmatic conception of social justice, typified by the Rawlsian maximin principle discussed in the Introduction, leads to the conclusion that the state should do nothing to redistribute income from capital to labor whether by direct or fiscal means: any attempt to reduce inequality would ultimately work against the least well off and would therefore not be just. The redistributive efforts of government should therefore be limited to reducing labor income inequality and forget about inequality between capital and labor.

This argument may be logically correct, but it is not confirmed by empirical studies. To measure the effects in question, economists rely on the notion of "elasticity of the supply of capital." If the rate of return on invested capital decreases by 1 percent, by how much does the supply of capital—that is, the quantity of savings that households decide to invest in firms—decrease? Empirical estimates of this elasticity find in general that it is fairly close to zero: when the return on capital decreases, households attempt to preserve future income by saving more, and in practice this seems to balance or even outweigh the fact that a lower return on investment makes immediate consumption more attractive than future consumption out of savings. In the jargon of economics, one says that the income effect compensates for the effect of substitution between present and future consumption (Atkinson and Stiglitz, 1980, chaps. 3–4). In fact, the high interest rates and reduced taxes on capital income seen in the 1980s and 1990s did not lead to unusually high rates of saving—quite the contrary. As long as the elasticity of capital supply is zero or close to it, that is, as long as the capital stock is relatively independent of the extent of redistribution, then fiscal redistribution permits, and social justice recommends, as extensive a redistribution as possible between capital and labor. If the elasticity of substitution between capital and labor is nonnegligible, such ambitious redistribution cannot be achieved efficiently through direct means, which, as discussed earlier, tend to reduce the level of employment unnecessarily.

It is true, however, that estimates of the elasticity of the supply of capital measure only some of the negative potential effects of redistribution, because in practice only part of investment comes directly from household savings. Another important, even predominant, part comes directly from the profits that firms do not distribute to shareholders and creditors. Relying on retained earnings is often more efficient than soliciting outside savings. Therefore, we must also take into account the effects of capital-labor redistribution on the financial structure of firms and their ability to invest out of earnings in order to arrive at a global estimate of the elasticity of the supply of capital and therefore at the optimal level of redistribution from the standpoint of social justice.

A more fundamental objection is that, even if the elasticity of the supply of capital is really low, taxation of capital income causes significant problems in a world in which savings and investment are internationally mobile and states choose their level of redistribution independently while attempting to attract as much investment capital as possible. Tax competition makes the supply of capital highly elastic for each state taken in isolation, even if the true elasticity of the global supply of capital is low. In fact, lack of coordination between governments largely accounts for the significant decrease in the taxation of capital in Europe in the 1980s and 1990s. Without fiscal federalism—or taxation of capital at the broadest possible geographical level—it is impossible to achieve an optimal redistribution from capital to labor in the social justice sense.

Are Capitalists and the Price System Necessary?

If one could precisely measure the elasticity of substitution between capital and labor and the elasticity of the supply of capital, it would be possible in principle to determine the optimal amount of capital-labor redistribution and the best instruments to achieve it. The intellectual and political conflict over redistribution is about more than just the measurement of elasticities, however. Indeed, this whole conceptual framework implicitly assumes that we accept the rules of the market economy and the allocative role of the price system. This is obvious in the case of the elasticity of capital supply (why should society give in to the threat of capitalist households to save less if they deem the rate of return on capital to be too low?). It is just as important, though, when it comes to the elasticity of capital/labor substitution: why should firms use more capital and less labor if the relative price

37

of labor rises? Wouldn't it be enough to prohibit firms from laying off workers, or simply to require firms to take into account the collective goals of high employment and social justice, subject to oversight by works councils and a vigilant public? To accept the allocative role of the price system and insist that fiscal redistribution is preferable to direct redistribution is tantamount to the claim that individual self-interest is the adequate guide to making correct resource allocation decisions in a complex economy. Traditionally, the left has rejected such fatalism and placed its faith in the possibility of organizing the economy in a more solidaristic way. Hence the left remains skeptical of taxation as the primary means of achieving social justice. In Chapter 3, we will see how this skepticism has influenced thinking about the redistribution of income from labor.

For now, consider the fact that this refusal to embrace the logic of the price system and of fiscal distribution (rather than belief in a low elasticity of capital-labor substitution) explains why much of the European left and trade-union movement was unenthusiastic toward, if not downright hostile to, the tax reform proposals of the 1980s and 1990s aimed at decreasing the tax burden on labor (such as the French CSG, as discussed earlier). These proposals were based on the idea that if labor is abundant, then a low price of labor and high price of capital may not be the worst way of encouraging firms to use less capital and more labor and encouraging consumers to consume more labor-intensive goods and fewer capital-intensive goods. How could it be otherwise in a world in which a wide range of different goods and services are produced, and it is difficult to determine the precise capital and labor content of each good? In other words, prices serve as a signal conveying information to various economic actors that would be difficult to convey in any other way, as illustrated by the universally acknowledged failure of central planning. But the issue is sufficiently complex, and the fatalistic acceptance of individual self-interest sufficiently depressing, that not everyone is willing to accept the logic of this argument.

The debate about the price system, individual self-interest, and other possible forms of economic organization, which raises questions that can never be fully answered on the basis of historical data alone, obviously stands on a different plane from the question of empirical estimates of the elasticity of the capital supply and capital/labor substitution, as well as on another plane from the controversy between classical and marginalist theory over the capital-labor split. Nevertheless, the two debates have not always been totally independent. As discussed above, a low elasticity of capital/labor substitution makes the price system less useful. If the capitalist mode of production is simply a mechanism for matching fixed quantities of capital and labor, n workers per machine, why is it necessary for anyone to own the machine? If the owner of the machine does nothing but claim a share of what it produces, then he could be eliminated by collectivizing the means of production. Saving could be replaced by taking a sufficient sum out of national income for the purpose of increasing the stock of machines and matching them to an appropriate number of workers: there would be no need of capitalists to accomplish this. This is obviously what Marx concluded from his observations of the capitalist economy, whose operation seemed terribly simple. Conversely, to insist on the possibility of substituting capital for labor, as marginalist economists do, is to emphasize the complexity of the modern economy and introduce the existence of choices, which someone must make, and this allows one to argue that the price system and private property are legitimate in the absence of some other system for solving complex problems of allocation. That is why the debate about capital/labor substitution has often been seen as a more general debate having to do with the legitimacy of capitalism and the price system, first in Marx's controversies with marginalist economists in the 1870s and later in the Cambridge capital controversy of the 1950s and 1960s.

Although this blurring of the boundaries between different debates is comprehensible, it is also unfortunate. The legitimacy of the price system is not simply a question of capital/labor substitutability, if only because the price system can play a useful role in deciding what goods and services to produce even if there is no possibility of substituting capital for labor. Conversely, as noted earlier, an answer to the question of capital/labor substitution cannot tell us what the optimal level of redistribution from capital to labor is. If we take the market economy as given, the real issue in the controversy between the classical theory and the marginalist theory of the capital-labor split is the issue of direct versus fiscal redistribution.

A Compromise between Short-Term and Long-Term Theories?

Can historical data, particularly concerning the capital-labor split, help to resolve the controversy between classical and marginalist theory?

It is not always easy to move back and forth between theoretical notions such as national income, profits and wages, or capital and labor and the empirical notions embodied in national accounting statistics (see box, "Measuring Capital's Share"). Once these difficulties are overcome, however, we observe a striking empirical regularity, which Keynes as early as 1930 regarded as the best-established regularity in all of economic science.

Indeed, Table 2.1 shows that the respective shares of profits and wages in the national income of three countries with very different histories, particularly in regard to social matters, remained more or less constant: the wage share never fell below 60 percent and never rose higher than 71 percent, generally hovering around 66–68 percent, and it is impossible to detect any systematic upward or downward trend. It appears that profits and wages always divide in such a way as to award one-third of national income to capital and two-thirds to labor.*

---

* On this apparent regularity, please see the Note to the Reader at the opening of this book; recent research calls it into question.

TABLE 2.1

*Capital and labor shares of value added in the United States, France,
and the United Kingdom from 1920 to 1995 (percent)*

| Year | United States | | France | | United Kingdom | |
	Capital	Labor	Capital	Labor	Capital	Labor
1920	35.2	64.8	33.7	66.3	38.1	61.9
1925	35.1	64.9	34.9	65.1	38.1	61.9
1930	37.9	62.1	32.5	67.5	38.1	61.9
1935	32.9	67.1	30.5	69.5	35.8	64.2
1940	36.9	63.1	31.3	68.7	36.3	63.7
1945	30.9	69.1				
1950	34.9	65.1	37.8	62.2	33.2	66.8
1955	34.9	65.1	34.1	65.9	32.5	67.5
1960	32.9	67.1	34.4	65.6	31.2	68.8
1965	35.9	64.1	32.4	67.6	32.5	67.5
1970	30.9	69.1	33.6	66.4	32.4	67.6
1975	30.9	69.1	29.7	70.3	28.3	71.7
1980	33.9	66.1	28.3	71.7	29.2	70.8
1985	34.0	66.0	32.0	68.0	32.2	67.8
1990	33.8	66.2	37.6	62.4	28.2	71.8
1995	33.5	66.5	39.7	60.3	31.5	68.5

Note: See box, "Measuring Capital's Share."

Sources: For 1980–1995: OECD, 1996, p. A27. For 1920–1975: United States, Atkinson, 1983, p. 202 and Duménil and Lévy, 1996, statistical appendix; France, INSEE, 1994, pp. 84–153 (author's calculations based on series cse, ebe, edve, and mse); United Kingdom, Atkinson, 1983, p. 201.

From Share of Value-Added to Household Income

Consider first the relation between this one-third–two-thirds split of income between capital and labor and the distribution of household income discussed in Chapter 1. Table 2.1 shows the split of primary income between labor and capital, that is, the sum of all wages

MEASURING CAPITAL'S SHARE

How does one measure the respective shares of profits and wages in total revenue? What a firm earns by selling its products to consumers and other firms goes to pay three different types of costs:

- The cost of intermediate consumption, that is, of goods and services the firm buys from other firms and consumes to produce its own goods and services, as opposed to the machinery and equipment that constitutes the firm's capital.

- The remuneration of workers, which includes net wages paid to workers, employee-paid social charges deducted from the worker's pay (gross wage = net wage + employee-paid social charges), and employer-paid social charges. This aggregate is equal to gross labor income, or, more simply, labor income.

- The remainder of the proceeds from sales (after the first two costs are deducted) is called the *gross operating surplus* (GOS). It is generally much higher than the firm's profit in the strict sense because the GOS goes to pay not only dividends to shareholders but also interest on loans, taxes on profits, and the replacement cost of worn machinery and equipment (depreciation of capital, or amortization). This aggregate represents the gross capital income, or, more simply, capital income.

The firm's value added is defined as the difference between the revenue from sales and the cost of intermediate consumption. The value added is thus equal to the sum of labor income and capital income. When we calculate the profit and wage shares, we calculate the share of capital income and labor income as percentages of value added. In other words, we deduct the cost of intermediate consumption. This is perfectly legitimate, since the cost of intermediate goods purchased from other firms goes to remunerate capital and labor in those firms, and we need to avoid double counting.

In addition to taxes levied directly on capital (such as tax on profits) and labor (such as social charges), which are included in capital and labor income, firms also pay indirect taxes such as the value-added tax, the amount of which does not depend directly on how value added is divided between capital and labor. Hence these taxes cannot be attributed to either gross capital income or gross labor income. In calculating the profit and wage shares, it is customary to omit these indirect taxes: in other words, we calculate these respective shares as a percentage of value added net of indirect taxes. Thus the sum of capital's share and labor's share equals 100 percent of net value added, as in Tables 2.1 and 2.2. This makes the results easier to interpret, since indirect taxes do not depend directly on the capital/labor split.

Finally, another complication has to do with the treatment of self-employment income (farmers, merchants, doctors, lawyers, and so on). Here, value added goes to pay both the labor of self-employed workers and the capital they have invested, even though their accounts do not clearly distinguish between wages and profits. Without correcting for self-employment income, one would find that the wage share of total value added has increased significantly since the nineteenth century, simply because the percentage of non-self-employed workers has increased so much (Morrisson, 1996, p. 78). The accounting convention used by the OECD is to attribute to self-employed workers the same average wage as non-self-employed workers. This convention has been applied to adjust the figures in Tables 2.1 and 2.2.

and other compensation, including employer-paid social charges (payroll taxes), effectively paid by firms to their workers, and the sum of gross profits or operating surpluses, that is, the residual revenue of firms after paying their workers (see box). The relation between this and disposable household income is complex. For example, a significant portion of the sums that appear in the "labor" column of Table 2.1 is paid in the form of social charges, which reappear in the form of pensions and social transfers in the disposable household income reported in Table 1.1. Furthermore, firms do not distribute all of their profits to the capitalist households that own their shares or bonds: a significant portion of firm profits, often more than half, is retained to compensate for the depreciation of capital (on average nearly 10 percent of value added) and to pay for new investments without having to seek outside capital.

Allowance must also be made for taxes paid by firms on their profits before distribution to shareholders. This factor is of limited importance, however, because although the tax on profits in most Western countries is on the order of 40–50 percent, receipts from this tax generally do not exceed 2.5–3 percent of GDP. In France in the 1990s, the figure was as low as 1.5 percent of GDP, even though the share of capital in value added was higher than elsewhere (OECD, 1995, p. 78). This is because the notion of taxable profits is much narrower than the notion of gross operating surplus, since firms are allowed to deduct not just the estimated depreciation of their capital stock but also the interest paid to creditors, provisions for anticipated risks, and so on. The tax on profits is by far the most riddled with loopholes in the whole tax system.

Note, finally, that a significant portion of the sums listed under "wages" in Table 1.1 are in fact paid by government entities out of revenue from the tax on profits or on total value added (in the form of a value-added tax, or VAT). This tends to increase the share of wages relative to capital income in total household income compared with the capital-labor split in the value added by firms. All these factors explain why, given gross profits on the order of 32–34 percent of value added by firms, the share of capital income actually received by households is typically only 10 percent of total household income (see Chapter 1).

What the Constancy of the Profit Share Tells Us

Consider once again Table 2.1. How should we interpret the constancy of the profit share across time and space? Leaving the matter of retained profits aside, the first lesson to be drawn from this regularity is that the considerable growth of workers' purchasing power in the twentieth century cannot be explained by changes in the capital-labor split. In other words, the reasons why the purchasing power of the French worker increased fourfold between 1920 and 1990 (see Table 1.6) was not that social conflict reduced the share of income appropriated by capitalists. Indeed, the share of wages in total value added was broadly speaking the same two-thirds of national income in 1920 as it was in 1990 (see Table 2.1). Furthermore, although the two world wars and changes in nomenclature make it difficult to extend statistical series on the profit/wage split beyond 1920 for France, we can use American statistics to go back all the way to 1869, and these indicate that the variation in the wage share was already limited to between 66 and 68 percent in the nineteenth century (Duménil and Lévy, 1996, chap. 15). In other words, the profit-wage split has remained almost constant for more than 120 years, even though wages increased tenfold.

To be sure, it is important that capital appropriated a third of value added throughout this period. If that income had all been distributed to labor, including the portion devoted to capital depreciation, wages could have been increased by 50 percent, which would have significantly improved the living conditions of workers in 1870 or even 1990, conditions that were in many cases miserable when compared with the opulence in which many capitalists lived. At the same time, however, we must admit that this 50 percent increase in wages would have been only half as much as the wage increase that actually occurred between 1870 and 1910 and less than a quarter as much as the increase that actually occurred between 1950 and 1994 (Table 1.6). It is difficult, moreover, to believe that the wage increases of 100 percent between 1870 and 1910 and more than 200 percent between 1950 and 1990 would have occurred if the capital share had been reduced to zero in 1870 or 1950. Although our knowledge on this point is limited, it is likely that the supply of capital would have decreased if there had been that much redistribution, hence that the optimal capital/labor redistribution from the standpoint of workers would have been much smaller, though surely larger than what was actually instituted.

Who Pays Social Charges (Payroll Taxes)?

The second lesson to draw from Table 2.1 has to do with the question of fiscal incidence. In the 1920s and 1930s firms paid little in the way of social charges, whereas in the 1990s 45 percent of the wage bill consisted of social charges paid by employers, while workers paid another 20 percent of their gross wages to support the welfare state (see box). Who actually bore the burden of employer-paid social charges? Certainly not the employers, since labor's share of value added, which includes employer-paid social charges, did not increase between 1920 and 1995. Similarly, employer-paid social charges were much lower in the United States and United Kingdom than in France in the 1990s, but labor's share of value added was no higher in France than in those two countries—indeed, the opposite was true (see Table 2.1). In 1996, the maximum rate of employer-paid social charges as a percentage of gross wages was 7.65 percent in the United States and 10.2 percent in the United Kingdom, with workers paying the same percentage, and total receipts from social charges (paid by both employers and employees) represented 6–7 percent of GDP, compared with nearly 20 percent of GDP in France (OECD, 1995, p. 79). If employer-paid charges were actually paid by employers, we would therefore expect to find that labor's share of value added in France was at least 10 percent of GDP higher than in the United States and United Kingdom.

It is therefore clear that social charges are not paid out of capital income. This is a crucial fact, since it implies that modern systems of social protection, which are central to today's systems of redistribution and which were based on the idea of dividing social costs between capitalists and workers, have not in fact redistributed income from capital to labor; labor income has absorbed the full cost. This in no way undermines the legitimacy of such systems, which do allow for considerable redistribution of labor income and fulfill an insurance function that private markets are often incapable of assuming (see Chapter 4). It does, however, profoundly challenge the implicit intention to redistribute income from capital to labor that in many cases informed the creation of the welfare state. This vision was closely linked to the classical theory of the capital-labor split, according to which a better division could be achieved through negotiation, for example, by setting a higher rate for employer payments than for employee payments: social benefits were thought of as a supplement to the wage that capitalists would otherwise have paid to workers.

In fact, the evidence appears to indicate that, as the theory of fiscal incidence would predict, the only thing one needs to know is how the tax is assessed, that is, how its amount depends on the level of wages, profits, and so on, and not what the name of the tax is or who is officially supposed to pay it, that is, who writes the check to the appropriate collection authority. It does not much matter whether social protection is paid for by an income tax proportionate to wages or by social charges levied on both employers and employees. In Denmark, there is no payroll tax, and the generous Danish system of social protection is financed entirely by income tax (which in practice is always mainly a tax on wages and social income in view of the limited importance of capital income). Unsurprisingly, the share of labor income in value added is the same in Denmark as elsewhere (OECD,

1996, p. A27). Danish firms spend as much as French firms on wages but pay it all to their workers instead of paying social charges; the workers then pay tax on their income. More generally, the share of social charges in the financing of European social protection systems varies widely from country to country, with France and Denmark representing the two extremes, but the share of labor in value added is more or less the same everywhere. The only relevant parameters are how the tax rate, whether assessed in the form of an income tax or a social contribution, depends on the wage level (in other words, how progressive is the assessment) and whether it also depends on the level of capital income. In particular, the only way to redistribute income from capital to labor is to tax capital.

A Cobb-Douglas Production Function?

With these lessons in mind, how can we explain the constancy of the share of profits? The interpretation traditionally favored by economists is that over the past century of capitalism, the Western economies have been reasonably well described at the macroeconomic level by a production function of the Cobb-Douglas type, which is to say, with an elasticity of capital/labor substitution equal to 1. Indeed, only if this elasticity is 1 can one confidently predict that the respective shares of profits and wages should remain constant over time regardless of changes in the available quantities of capital and labor and regardless of political and economic shocks affecting the price of each factor. An elasticity of 1 would also explain the observed fiscal incidence of social contributions, whose burden falls on labor and therefore increases its price.

Even with a fixed-coefficient technology, one could of course argue that social and political conflict always leads to the same result in all countries, with one-third of income going to capital and two-thirds to labor. As Solow himself has noted, we would need to know how much variation it would be natural to expect before describing the constancy of the capital-labor split as surprising (Solow, 1958). Econometricians have looked at how hiring by individual firms varies in response to variations in the price of labor, however, and these micro-economic studies show considerable elasticity of substitution between capital and labor. After comparing the results of several dozen studies across all Western countries, Hamermesh (1986; 1993) found that most estimates of the demand elasticity for labor suggest elasticities of substitution between capital and labor of 0.7 to 1.1, leading to the conclusion that "the Cobb-Douglas function seems to be a fairly good approximation to reality" (1986, pp. 451–452, 467). Contrasting experience in various Western countries since the 1970s also suggests substantial capital/labor substitutability (I will return to this point later). The data thus seem to confirm the marginalist theory of the capital-labor split and therefore the superiority of fiscal redistribution over direct redistribution.

Historical Time versus Political Time?

One should be careful not to underestimate the limits of this historical regularity, however. Although the profit share of income is impressively constant over the long run, it does vary over the short run, and the long run can seem very long indeed to the individuals affected. Consider, for instance, the evolution of respective shares of profits and wages in the OECD countries between 1979 and 1995.

Tables 2.1 and 2.2 show large variations in the profit and wage shares. Although the wage share tended to increase in the 1970s, it was the profit share that increased in the 1980s and 1990s, in some cases substantially. These variations were widest in France, where the wage share was 66.4 percent in 1970, rising to 71.8 percent in 1981, then falling after 1982 to 62.4 percent in 1990 and 60.3 percent in 1995. How can we explain the fact that more than 5 percent of national income was redistributed from capital to labor between 1970 and 1982, while 10 percent went from labor to capital between 1983 and 1995?

It so happens that the first period coincides with a period of substantial wage increases inaugurated by the Grenelle Accords of 1968.

TABLE 2.2

Capital's share in value added in the OECD
from 1979 to 1995 (percent)

Year	Germany	United States	France	Italy	United Kingdom	OECD
1979	30.5	35.0	30.0	35.5	31.3	32.8
1980	28.5	33.9	28.3	36.0	29.2	32.2
1981	28.2	34.5	28.2	35.3	28.9	32.1
1982	28.6	33.6	28.5	35.4	30.7	31.8
1983	30.8	33.3	29.2	34.5	32.3	32.2
1984	31.8	34.0	30.7	36.4	31.9	33.2
1985	32.4	34.0	32.0	36.6	32.2	33.7
1986	33.1	34.0	34.9	38.6	31.0	34.1
1987	32.7	33.2	35.5	38.4	31.4	33.8
1988	33.8	33.1	36.9	38.8	30.9	34.2
1989	34.6	34.4	38.1	38.3	29.6	34.9
1990	35.6	33.8	37.6	37.3	28.2	34.5
1991	34.0	33.3	37.9	36.6	26.8	33.9
1992	33.3	33.6	38.2	36.6	27.7	34.0
1993	33.4	33.6	37.8	36.9	29.9	34.2
1994	35.0	33.8	39.4	39.8	31.0	34.8
1995	36.0	33.5	39.7	42.5	31.5	35.0

Note: See box, "Measuring Capital's Share."
  Source: OECD, 1996, p. A27.

Wages continued to improve in the 1970s owing to the influence of social movements and substantial increases in the minimum wage. The last major increment to the minimum wage occurred in 1981. After 1983, wages ceased to be indexed to prices, and increases to the minimum wage were minimal. In fact, the purchasing power of the average net wage increased 53 percent between 1968 and 1983 but only 8 percent between 1983 and 1995 (INSEE, 1996a, p. 48). True, GDP increased 44 percent between 1970 and 1983 but only 28 percent between 1983 and 1995 (INSEE, 1996c, p. 34), and this growth had to finance a growing burden of pension and health care expenditures, but the reduction of wage growth relative to national income growth was nevertheless quite real. In other words, over a period of twenty-five years, the predictions of the classical theory of the capital-labor split seemed to be accurate: the profit share decreased when social militancy enabled workers to win important concessions on wages, and it increased when constraints were imposed on wages. Yet the increased profit share did not lead to the promised creation of new jobs.

To be sure, these substantial variations over a twenty-five-year period do not change the fact that over periods of fifty or a hundred years, wages have always accounted for roughly two-thirds of added value, so that the increase in workers' purchasing power of 250 percent since 1950 and 700 percent since 1870 cannot be explained by changes in the capital-labor split. But why would that matter to the workers who lived through the twenty-five years from 1970 to 1995? Their standard of living increased sharply from 1968 to 1982 and then stagnated from 1983 to 1995 while output continued to grow. How could they not associate the improvement in their standard of living with redistribution from capital to labor? The right-wing view that true improvement in the standard of living can come only from growth and not from redistribution is valid only in the long run, and politics, in which workers have a legitimate interest, operates on a different time scale.

Furthermore, how could workers fail to associate redistribution from capital to labor with social struggles and wage increases and thus with direct rather than fiscal redistribution? Indeed, no fiscal redistribution had ever redistributed 10 percent of national income in so short a period. To give an order of magnitude, the fiscal redistribution measures adopted by the Socialist government after it came to power in France in 1981, which were denounced at the time by the right as the height of "fiscal bludgeoning" and which consisted essentially of a wealth tax and a surtax on top income brackets, brought in less than 10 billion francs in 1981 (Nizet, 1990, pp. 402, 433), or 0.3 percent of national income. In theory, a government can achieve any level of redistribution it wants via taxes and transfers, but in practice no transfer of comparable magnitude has been accomplished in so few years. Inevitably, therefore, workers think of and experience redistribution primarily in terms of social struggle and wage increases rather than fiscal reform and transfer payments. It is not so much rejection of the logic of fiscal redistribution and the price system that sustains left-wing skepticism of redistribution through taxation; it is rather this historical reality. We will again encounter this same historical reality and contrast between historical and political time in the discussion of inequality of labor income in Chapter 3.

This level of variation in the capital-labor split over a period of ten to fifteen years is not historically unique, moreover, even if certain specific features of French social and political history helped make the period 1970–1990 particularly noteworthy. For instance, the share of wages in the value added by American firms decreased from about 65 to 55 percent between 1869 and 1880, then rose again to 65 percent in 1885 and to 66–68 percent in 1890. The average wage rose by only 2 percent between 1869 and 1880 but then increased 27 percent between 1880 and 1885, a period marked by major strikes and an unusually active trade-union movement (Duménil and Lévy, 1996, chap. 16). Over a period of ten to fifteen years, the marginalist understanding of the capital-labor split can frequently seem rather absurd in the light of social realities. The same can be said about the question of fiscal incidence: in the short term, social charges assessed on employers are indeed paid by the employers and are not immediately nullified by wage reductions, a fact that inevitably shapes the way many people see fiscal incidence, even though it is true that over the long run social charges always end up being paid by labor.

*Why Has the Profit Share Not Increased in the United States
and United Kingdom?*

When it comes to the history of the capital-labor split in the period
1970–2000, things are not so simple, however. The French pattern was
reproduced in Italy, where the profit share rose from 34.5 percent in
1983 to 42.5 percent in 1995, and to a slightly lesser extent in Germany,
where it rose from 28.2 percent in 1981 to 36 percent in 1995. Strikingly,
however, the United States and United Kingdom seem to have entirely
avoided this increase in the profit share in the 1980s and 1990s: the
wage share of US value added held steady at 66–67 percent throughout
this period, while in Britain it remained between 68 and 71 percent
(Table 2.2). It is difficult to compare profit shares at different points
in time between different countries because of numerous differences
in accounting conventions, but comparing trends over time leaves no
doubt: the capital share increased by nearly 10 percent of value added
in France, Italy, and Germany, whereas it did not increase at all in the
United States and United Kingdom. In contrast to what happened
with wage inequality, which increased sharply in the United States and
United Kingdom after 1970 (see Chapter 1), the countries where ultra-
liberalism won out in the 1980s and 1990s are the only countries in
which the profit share did not increase. How do we explain this?

Part of the explanation is surely that there was catching-up to do:
in France, the profit share had decreased by 5–6 percent of value added
in the 1970s owing to very rapid wage increases. In the United
Kingdom, the profit share decrease was much more moderate, and in
the United States it did not occur at all (Table 2.1). This cannot be the
whole story, however: by 1985–1986, the profit share in France had returned to its 1970 level, yet it continued to increase, while the profit
share in the United States and United Kingdom remained stable.

It is hard to avoid relating this to the fact that the United States
and United Kingdom were the only two countries to have created jobs

in this period, thus increasing their total wage bill, while wages stagnated in the other countries. Between 1983 and 1996, the United States created 25 million jobs, an increase of about 25 percent (from 100.8 million to 126.4 million), while total employment in France increased by barely 2 percent (from 21.9 million to 22.3 million), and GDP in both the United States and France increased by about 30 percent (OECD, 1996, p. A23). This is surely the best proof that capital and labor can be combined in different proportions to increase production by the same amount, hence that there is considerable opportunity for substitution at the macroeconomic level. Between 1983 and 1996, the French economy grew by employing skilled labor together with new machinery and infrastructure, while American growth relied on intensive use of labor, especially relatively unskilled labor in the service sector (restaurants, commerce. etc.) (Piketty, 1997b). This interpretation is confirmed, moreover, by available data concerning the growth of the capital stock in the period 1970–2000, which show that it grew much more rapidly in France and most other European countries than in the United States (IMF, 1996). The data also show the degree to which capital/labor substitution can be related to major intersectoral reallocations (from industry to services, for example), and not just substitution of workers for machines at the firm or sector level.

The simplest explanation might be that labor was not substituted for capital in France, and jobs were not created, because wages were too high owing to very rapid wage growth in the period 1968–1983. This would suggest that the long run, in which the effects of marginalist theory would manifest themselves, is not as far off as the individuals involved might have hoped. In order for lower wages to lead to more jobs, however, the job creation effect would have to outweigh the wage effect, that is, the elasticity of substitution between labor and capital would have to be greater than 1, which, as mentioned, is higher than the usual estimates. Furthermore, if the average wage in the United States rose by barely 5 percent between 1983 and 1996, it increased by nearly 20 percent in the United Kingdom, compared with less than

12 percent in France, yet total employment in Britain increased by nearly 10 percent in the same period (OECD, 1996, A15, A19, A23). In the period 1983–1996, France thus appears to have lost across the board, since wages and jobs stagnated, leading to an exceptionally large decrease in labor's share of value added.

In addition to the average cost of labor, two other factors might explain why the wage share decreased in France and continental Europe while holding steady in the United States and United Kingdom. One explanation might be that the variation of wages with skill level increased in the United States and United Kingdom, and that this was the sole explanation of employment growth in the 1980s and 1990s (see Chapter 3). A second possible interpretation is that labor income includes a nonmonetary component in the form of stability and guaranteed employment, and this component decreased in the United States and United Kingdom but remained high in France and elsewhere in Europe (see Cohen et al., 1996 for a comparison of France and the United States). We would then need to explain why the price of this employment guarantee should have increased between 1970 and 1995, and compare this to the incontestably high value placed on it by workers.

The Dynamics of the Distribution of Capital

Why does capital/labor inequality command so much attention? Not just because capital claims a significant share of national income. Even more striking is the fact that capital/labor inequality often reproduces itself or even grows over time. It is this reproduction that makes capital/labor inequality seem arbitrary, useless, and incompatible not only with common sense and social justice but also with economic efficiency: Why should capital-poor individuals or countries be denied the possibility to invest to the extent their talents permit? In other words, capital/labor inequality immediately raises the question of efficient (as opposed to pure) redistribution. The time has come, therefore, to move from the macroeconomic division of total income between the two factors of production, labor and capital, to the study of the income distribution at the individual level. What are the dynamics underlying changes in the income of individual workers and capitalists, and what investment opportunities are open to them? Does the logic of the market economy lead to an inefficient reproduction of inequality in the distribution of capital over time? If so, how can it be prevented?

The Theory of Perfect Credit and Convergence

Once again we have dueling theories. The central question has to do with the credit market. If the credit market were perfectly efficient, that is, if capital were invested wherever a profitable investment opportunity existed, then any initial inequality in the distribution of capital should eventually cease to exist. No matter how wealthy a family or country is initially, all equally enterprising units of labor would then be able to make the same investments thanks to the credit market. Hence the inequality of initial endowments would not persist. Of course, even in a perfect credit market, a poor person or country that borrows to invest must eventually repay the loan and therefore cannot instantly save enough to close the wealth gap between borrower and lender. In fact, if the savings rate of low-income earners is lower than that of high-income earners, the inequality between borrower and lender can persist indefinitely (Bourguignon, 1981). At the international level, this would correspond to a situation in which per capita GDP is the same in all countries, since an equal quantity of capital is invested per worker everywhere, but GNP is lower in poor countries, where the capital is owned by the rich countries and which must therefore pay a share of their profits every year to capitalists in other countries. But if borrowers save at the same (or nearly the same) rate as lenders, they can gradually accumulate the fruits of their labor, borrow less and less, and eventually catch up. In fact, savings rates are not systematically lower for low-income countries than for high-income countries: they were above 30 percent in the Asian "tigers" in the 1950s and 1960s and below 10–15 percent in all Western countries in the 1980s and 1990s, even though the latter were much wealthier than the former; that is why these developing countries were able to catch up with the rich countries (Young, 1995).

Convergence of the rich and poor countries is the principal prediction of the standard model of growth and capital accumulation (Solow, 1956), which assumes perfect credit markets. What justifies this assumption? If you believe in market forces, the answer is simple: competition. Why would a bank or wealthy capitalist not lend to someone with a profitable investment project who promises to pay a competitive rate of interest? If the problem faced by poor countries is lack of machinery and infrastructure, then new investment should enable them to increase their output considerably. What could prevent rich countries from using their savings to profit from such investment? If some potential lenders are nervous or hesitant, what is to prevent others from taking advantage of the opportunity? The perfect credit model thus depends on competition among savers and financial intermediaries to identify the most profitable investment opportunities. It follows immediately that redistribution from those well endowed with capital to those less well endowed can be justified solely on grounds of pure social justice. If this is correct, then the unequal distribution of capital as such poses no inherent problem of economic efficiency, because the market would see to it that the available capital would be invested efficiently (in the Pareto sense, as discussed in the Introduction). No direct intervention in the production process would be required.

The Question of Convergence between Rich and Poor Countries

The convergence model leads to some particularly striking predictions at the international level. If investment capability does not vary systematically from one country to another, we should expect to see a

57

global catch-up phenomenon. Capital should flow to poor countries, increasing their rate of growth, thus reducing and eventually eliminating inequality between countries. That is the theory. What do we see in practice?

A comparison of per capita income with growth rate for a sample of countries in the period 1960–1990 fails to confirm the theoretical prediction: there is no systematic relation between the two variables (Mankiw et al., 1992, p. 427). Some Asian countries that were relatively poor in 1960, such as Taiwan, South Korea, and Singapore, did see higher growth rates of per capita income than Western countries, but other poor countries, such as those on the Indian subcontinent or in sub-Saharan Africa, experienced very low or even negative rates of growth. The convergence model seems to explain catch-up among the Western countries themselves: for example, the countries of Western Europe closed the gap with the United States after World War II. It also accounts for the rapid growth of Asian countries with intermediate levels of per capita income, which also moved closer to the more advanced economies. But it does not help us to understand the relation between the richest countries and the poorest or between the rich countries and the middle-of-the-pack countries of South America, both cases in which the gap has widened. A similar conclusion would probably hold true over longer periods—if it were possible, for example, to measure correctly the income gap between developed and underdeveloped countries since the nineteenth century (Morrisson, 1996, p. 181). In fact, not only did the rich countries fail to invest massively in poorer countries, but the exact opposite occurred: broadly speaking, we see a net flow of capital from the poorest countries to the richest (Lucas, 1990b), because capitalists in the poor countries invest more in the rich countries than the other way around.

Just because capital has not been invested in the poor countries, which have remained poor, it does not follow that credit market imperfections are solely responsible. If, for instance, we control for the "initial stock of human capital" in 1960 (as measured by literacy rates, educational levels, and so on), we find that there is a negative correlation between initial per capita income in 1960 and average growth rate in the period 1960–1990. Endogenous growth theorists refer to this as "conditional" convergence as opposed to the "unconditional" convergence predicted by the Solow model (Mankiw et al., 1992). For example, South American countries with the same per capita income as the Asian tigers in 1960 had a much lower stock of human capital, because large segments of the population had been totally neglected, whereas in Asia inequality was much lower. These countries grew much more slowly than the Asian tigers, which were able to catch up with the West. In addition to human capital, initial inequality also had a negative effect on future growth, whether directly or indirectly (owing to social and political instability due to inequality) (Benabou, 1996).

Another lesson from the experience of the Asian tigers is the importance of global market integration. The miraculous growth formula (based on high and relatively egalitarian investment in human capital on the one hand and economic liberalization and openness to foreign markets on the other) appears to have spread in the 1980s and 1990s to larger Asian countries. The fact that liberalization has been less successful in India than in China reminds us, however, of the crucial importance of the egalitarian element, without which liberalization cannot lead to lasting growth (Drèze and Sen, 1995). Egalitarian educational policies are probably the most basic example of efficient redistribution (see Chapter 3).

As Robert Lucas (1990b) has shown, moreover, if the difference in per capita income between the United States and India were explicable solely by different endowments in machinery, infrastructure, and so on, one would have to conclude that the marginal productivity of capital in India is 58 times higher in India than in the United States. With that much of a difference in the return on capital invested in India, it is difficult to see what kind of credit market imperfection could account for the failure of Western capital to take advantage of the opportunity. We must therefore yield to the evidence, which shows that a substantial portion of the inequality between the rich and poor countries, and indeed of inequality in general, is due not to unequal distribution of the means of production but to unequal distribution of human capital: the fact that nearly 50 percent of the Indian population is illiterate surely reduces by a substantial amount the return on an additional unit of capital invested in India (Drèze and Sen, 1995, table A1).

The Problem of Capital Market Imperfections

Just because other factors influence growth, however, it does not follow that capital flows from the rich to the poor countries are not important. The absence of substantial flows from the rich to poor countries reminds us of the chronic weakness of international capital flows in general. In the West, for example, the available amount of domestic savings is closely related to the annual level of domestic investment, whereas we would not expect this to be the case if international financial markets were truly integrated, allowing domestic investments to be made with imported capital even in the absence of domestic savings.

In contrast to what the perfect credit market model assumes, a credit operation is more than just a mechanical placement of capital where there was none, in exchange for which the lender or investor receives a portion of the profits. In practice, the lender or investor has to make sure that the proposed project is profitable and that the level of risk is acceptable. The borrower will of course always claim that it is. The lender will also want to make sure that the borrower has sufficient incentives to do what needs to be done over a long period of time even though some of the gains will go to the lender. Finally, the lender needs to assure himself that the borrower will not simply disappear with the profits. Investment thus raises a series of problems that economists have classified as problems of "adverse selection" and "moral hazard." Such problems arise wherever there is an "intertemporal" market, that is, a market in which exchanges occur in different time periods. Credit markets are intertemporal markets, as are social insurance markets, which we will encounter in Chapter 4. These problems are particularly difficult in international markets, because the information available about potential borrowers and investment projects in another country may be of low quality. This is why international capital flows are much lower than they might be.

Is competition the least harmful way to solve the informational problems that markets and governments face? In practice, the only thing lenders can really do to make sure they will recover their principal is to demand that the borrower put up collateral, or, equivalently, that the borrower invest his own capital initially in order to establish a credible commitment to the venture and a token of confidence in its viability. Hence the amount that an individual or firm can borrow to finance an investment depends on his (or its) initial wealth. As the French saying has it, *"on ne prête qu'aux riches"* (one lends only to the rich). This is an efficient mechanism from the standpoint of lenders but inefficient for society as a whole: total income could be higher if capital were redistributed in such a way as to enable financing of all profitable investments. The imperfection of the credit market is a prime example of the kind of market imperfection that can be used to justify redistribution on grounds of economic efficiency and not just pure social justice. In principle, it should be possible to allocate resources more efficiently while achieving a more equitable distribution of wealth (see the Introduction).

Many critics of capitalism, starting with the socialist theorists of the nineteenth century, have long been aware of the phenomenon of credit rationing, even if many considered it so obvious that they saw no need to analyze it or even mention it. It is only since the 1970s, however, that economic theorists have begun to analyze the basic reasons for this capital market imperfection and its consequences for redistribution (Piketty 1994, pp. 774–779). The latter extend beyond the fact that total income could be increased by redistributing capital. When credit rationing exists, for example, the choice of what individuals do—whether they choose self-employment or paid labor for someone else, for example—depends on their initial wealth, so that a redistribution of wealth can have long-term implications for the occupational structure and for growth, as shown by a comparison of the relatively egalitarian distribution in France after the Revolution with the inegalitarian distribution at the time of the Industrial Revolution in Britain (Banerjee and Newman, 1993).

Possible Public Interventions

What kinds of public intervention would help to combat credit rationing and the persistence of capital/labor inequality to which it can lead? The principal problem faced by possible interventions is the same as that which gives rise to credit rationing in the first place: investing is not simply a matter of placing capital where there is none. Complex choices have to be made, involving what sectors to invest in, what goods to produce, and what people should be empowered to make these decisions. The difficulties are obvious when we look at the radical solution of abolishing private ownership of capital and collectivizing the means of production. Doing so does nothing to resolve the problems of creating incentives and allocating resources. Other historical experiments with efficient redistribution have faced similar difficulties: these include public investment banks, subsidized loans, and, in poor countries, development banks. Indeed, the theory of credit rationing tells us that it is just as difficult for a public bank as for a private bank to make sure that capital is correctly invested when the equivalent of a market rate of interest is to be deducted from the borrower's eventual profits. If the intention is to make a gift to the borrower by charging less than the market rate of interest, as is often implicitly the case with public investment banks and other subsidized forms of credit, it is not obvious that a public agency, no matter how well intentioned, can correctly decide which borrowers to favor, which sectors deserve additional investment, and so on. These very real difficulties arrive whenever a rich country seeks to transfer wealth to a poor country. Where should foreign aid go? How can one make sure that good use is made of it? Capital redistribution is not a matter of dropping capital from a helicopter into places where there isn't any. In practice, it is much easier to allow labor to move from places where capital is in short supply to places where there is lots of it: unlike capital, labor can integrate itself into the production process.

In fact, experiments with administered credit have often failed. Many development banks have made considerable losses without producing a visible return on investment or increased output. In Western countries, there is great skepticism about the utility of subsidized loans and public credit, at least since the 1980s.

Agriculture is the only realm in which direct redistribution of capital has met with tangible success. For example, since 1960, some development banks (such as the Grameen Bank in Bangladesh) specializing in loans to poor rural households that were excluded from the traditional banking system have enabled millions of peasants to obtain equipment and increase their productivity, inspiring similar experiments throughout the world. Agrarian reforms aimed at redistributing land or securing the leases of poor peasant farmers have often led to important gains in productivity, in Bengal for example (Banerjee and Ghatak, 1995).

These significant increases in productivity show the importance of capital market imperfections: a perfect credit market would have given credit to peasants to enable them to become landowners and improve their productivity. The problem is obviously that these productivity gains could not have been achieved if the peasant's motivation had been reduced by having to pay back a loan. Redistribution was the only way to motivate the peasants to improve their productivity. These successful experiments should be compared with the disastrous results of the collectivization of farming in the Soviet Union. It is easy to explain why redistribution of privately owned capital worked well in agriculture, because in the agricultural sector the problems of allocation and investment are less difficult to solve than elsewhere. It is enough to give each peasant enough land to increase his incentive to produce and innovate above what it was when the land was controlled by a landlord or collective farm.

A Flat Tax on Capital?

In order to redistribute capital efficiently where credit rationing exists, one therefore needs to find tools as transparent and unbiased as possible so as to avoid the pitfalls of administered credit. Historically, the imposition of progressive taxes on income and inheritance has greatly contributed to reducing the concentration of capital (as noted in Chapter 1). More generally, one could envision the imposition of a general tax on wealth: on coming of age, each citizen would receive a check to be invested in whatever way he or she deems most profitable. Of course there would obviously be costs associated with any such permanent redistribution of wealth, since it would inevitably discourage future accumulation. But those costs should be compared with the benefits obtained by financing profitable investments that would not otherwise be made. The traditional argument that the costs of a capital tax in terms of reduced long-term accumulation always outweigh the benefits ceases to be true when capital markets are imperfect (Chamley, 1996). Everything therefore depends on the quantitative importance of the profitable investments that go unfinanced owing to the capital market failure. Should wealth be taxed at a rate of 1 percent or 5 percent or 0.1 percent? In order to answer this question, one would need reliable estimates of the quantity of unfinanced but profitable investment opportunities, estimates that are very difficult to come by. Furthermore, between zealous proponents of perfect credit markets, for whom the unequal distribution of capital raises no problem of efficiency, and radical critics of capitalism, for whom the problem can be solved only by the abolition of private property, a climate of civil war has long since reigned, and this has discouraged the accumulation of knowledge in this nevertheless important area.

To sum up, there is clearly no shortage of justifications for a transparent redistribution of capital and its income. The case can be made purely in terms of social justice, in order to achieve a true redistribution of income between capital and labor, as opposed to the illusory redistribution created by employer social charges. Or it can be made in terms of economic efficiency, in order to combat the negative effects of capital market imperfections. In practice, efforts at capital/labor redistribution in the twentieth century have been disastrous not only in countries that tried to abolish private ownership of capital, where workers' living standards stagnated while improving rapidly in the capitalist countries, but also in the West, where a very small fraction of the tax burden actually falls on capital. These unsatisfactory outcomes show why the choice of instruments for achieving redistribution is so important. It is not enough merely to want to redistribute; adequate instruments are also necessary. These historical experiences, coupled with the objective difficulty of taxing capital income (which is often hard to monitor because of the many forms of investment and their high degree of mobility), suggest that a significant improvement could be achieved with an easily calculated tax designed to end the dramatic hemorrhage of taxable assets that we observe in practice. This tax should be applied to all forms of capital income over as broad a geographical area as possible in order to avoid the negative effects of fiscal competition between states. The instrument I have in mind is a *flat tax* (that is, a universal tax with a single rate). Although such a tax is not well suited to fiscal redistribution of labor income, which requires greater flexibility (see Chapter 4), it might well be suited to dealing with capital income in today's world.

THREE

Inequality of Labor Income

Although it is often thought that capital income is very unequally distributed while labor income is not, the fact is that the lion's share of income inequality today (and probably for a long time in the past) is due to labor income inequality. For instance, it is the increase in labor income inequality that is responsible for the reversal of the Kuznets curve that has taken place since the 1970s: in the United States, the gap between the top and bottom 10 percent of the income distribution has increased by nearly 50 percent. In order to understand inequality as it presently exists and redistribution as it might exist in the future, we must therefore give up the idea that labor incomes are relatively equal and that inequality exists primarily between capital and labor. Instead, we need to analyze the reasons for labor income inequality. The point of such analysis is to determine what kinds of redistributive instruments might combat it. The goal is no longer to abolish private ownership of capital, tax profits, or redistribute wealth. The instruments suitable for dealing with labor income inequality go by other names: taxation of top incomes and fiscal transfers to those with lower incomes; policies to improve education and training; minimum wages; and measures to prevent employment discrimination, strengthen unions, and establish wage schedules, to name a few. Which of these instruments are the most justifiable? What arguments are invoked to justify (or reject) them, and how are we to evaluate such arguments?

Inequality of Wages and Human Capital

The simplest theory of wage inequality is that different workers contribute different amounts to a firm's output. The computer specialist who develops a program for analyzing a firm's customer records quickly and efficiently is worth more to the firm than the office worker who processes a certain number of files each day, and that is why the firm pays the computer specialist more, lest competitors hire her away. Call this the theory of human capital. It has long met with hostility. Why? No doubt because a theory that declares that a computer specialist is worth more than an office worker because she brings more human capital and therefore greater productivity to the firm is often suspected of suggesting that this inequality of human capital actually measures an irremediable inequality between two human beings and may even be used to justify a considerable difference in standards of living. These suspicions are not totally illegitimate, moreover, since it was Gary Becker and his colleagues at the University of Chicago, known for their ultrafree market position, who developed and popularized the theory (Becker, 1964). Of course, economists do not limit themselves to explaining wage inequality by individual productivity. They also try to explain the origins of human capital inequality and propose a theory of education and training that leads to rejection of any ambitious form of public intervention.

It is nevertheless useful to examine these various questions separately, in order to distinguish, as discussed in the Introduction, between pure redistribution (in the form of transfers from high earners to low earners) and efficient redistribution (in the form of interventions in the process of human capital formation). We begin, therefore, by taking inequality of human capital as a given. Can observed wage inequality be explained solely in terms of differences of productivity? What does observed wage inequality tell us about the most efficient way of remedying the unequal standards of living that result from unequal wages? We will then turn to the question of human capital formation. Where does human capital inequality come from, and what instruments would enable us to change it in an efficient way?

The Explanatory Power of the Theory of Human Capital

In its most rudimentary form (that is, ignoring the question of the origins of inequality), the theory of human capital simply states that labor is not a homogeneous entity and that for various reasons different individuals are characterized by different endowments of human capital, that is, by different capacities to contribute to the production of goods and services demanded by consumers. Given some distribution of human capital within the population of workers and the demand for various goods and for the human capital needed to produce them (the demand for labor), then the laws of supply and demand determine the wages associated with each level of human capital and thus the distribution of labor income. The notion of human capital is therefore quite general, because it includes credentials such as diplomas, experience, and, more generally, individual characteristics that influence a worker's ability to participate in the production process for the demanded variety of goods and services. Can this theory account for the observed inequality of labor income?

Important Historical Inequalities

At this level of generality, the theory of human capital seems inevitable if one wants to explain the high degree of wage inequality that we observe across time and space. The fact that the average wage in the developed countries in 1990 was ten times what it was in 1870, as noted in Chapter 1, cannot be explained solely by the fact that workers in 1990 were so much more skilled than in 1870 that they could produce ten times more in the same period. What alternative explanation might exist, since we saw that labor's share in value added was the same in 1990 as in 1870, so that the increase in wages was not a result of a decrease in the share of profits (see Chapter 2)? Over the long run, it is undeniable that the marked increase in the purchasing power of workers was due to an increase in the productivity of labor.

68

Similarly, we saw that if one tries to explain why the purchasing power of workers in less-developed countries is one-tenth what it is in developed countries, the fact that the vast majority of workers in the developed countries have completed secondary education, while 50 percent of those in the less-developed countries are illiterate, surely plays a key role. Other factors, such as the imperfection of the credit market, which deprives workers in less-developed countries of sufficient investment capital, as well as closed borders, which prevent them from benefiting from the physical and human capital in the developed countries, aggravate this inequality even more. Still, it is significant inequality in the productivity of labor that inevitably accounts for wage inequality between the North and South.

Supply and Demand

Human capital theory is also indispensable for explaining the less spectacular but still striking inequalities that exist within a single country over a shorter period of time. For example, the average wage of a skilled worker to that of an unskilled worker in the United Kingdom was 2.4 in 1815, rose to 3.8 in 1851, and thereafter decreased steadily to 2.5 in 1911 (Williamson, 1985). Why was this ratio 60 percent higher in the middle of the nineteenth century than at the beginning and end? The most convincing explanation, confirmed by various sources, is that during the first half of the nineteenth century, the growing mechanization of industry considerably increased the demand for skilled labor, while at the same time an increase of agricultural productivity led to a substantial rural exodus that rapidly increased the supply of unskilled labor. In the second phase, the influx of unskilled labor from the countryside leveled off while apprenticeships rapidly increased the supply of skilled labor, so that the gap between the average wages of the two groups began to decrease. Similarly, although on a smaller scale, it has been shown that the gap between the average wage of workers with only a high school diploma or less and that of workers who continued their studies after high school decreased by roughly 15 percent between 1970 and 1980 in the United States before rising by more than 25 percent between 1980 and 1990 (Murphy and Welch, 1993a,b, p. 106). The decreased gap in the 1970s is all the more striking in that it occurred at a time when wage inequalities in general were increasing. Now, it so happens that the growth rate of the population of workers with post–high school education attained its historic high in the 1970s as the baby boom generation completed its education and entered the job market; subsequently, this growth rate diminished substantially.

These two examples are important, because reversals of wage gaps of this magnitude are seldom seen. In both cases, changes in the relative supply of and demand for different levels of human capital provide reasonably satisfactory explanations of the observed changes.

The Rise of Wage Inequality since 1970

Can supply and demand also account for the general increase of wage inequality (and the other labor-related inequalities discussed in Chapter 1) in a number of Western countries since 1970? Many economists have sought to explain rising inequality by shifts in the supply and demand of human capital over the long run. During the first phase of the Industrial Revolution, they argue, wage inequality increased as industry demanded more and more skilled labor and large numbers of unskilled laborers streamed in from the countryside. From the end of the nineteenth century to the 1970s, wage inequality decreased in all the developed countries. The phase of decreasing inequality occurred because skill gaps narrowed considerably thanks to rapid development of mass education and training, and growing demand for industrial workers with mid-level skills. Since the beginning of deindustrialization in the late 1960s, however, a new phase has ostensibly begun. New sectors (such as business services, computers, and communications) require workers with very high skill levels, but much of the population has been unable to acquire these skills through either the educational system or personal experience. These relatively unskilled workers find work in low-productivity sectors (such as personal services, the food service industry, and retailing) or else find themselves unemployed or underemployed. More extreme versions of the theory take this argument even further, arguing that wage inequality has risen not simply because the educational system has not kept up with the demand for human capital from new sectors and new technologies (as was the case in the first half of the nineteenth century), but rather because technological progress has placed a premium on individual qualities that have always been unequally distributed. These innate inequalities went unnoticed earlier, however, because traditional technologies made more routine demands and did not require these higher-level talents. This hypothesis goes by the name "skill-biased technological change" (Juhn et al., 1993).

Skill-Biased Technological Change?

At first glance, this theory of the long-term evolution of wage inequality in the West seems fairly plausible, at least in its less extreme forms. In the United States, the first country affected by these changes, one does find an increase in wage inequalities linked to skill: since 1980, the effects of a year of additional study, a higher-level diploma, or length of professional experience on average pay have increased noticeably. In the jargon of labor economists, the "return" to skill has increased (Juhn et al., 1993).

The problem is that roughly 60 percent of the overall increase in wage inequality has occurred within groups of workers who share the same observable characteristics: the same level of education, length of professional experience, and age (Juhn et al., 1993, p. 431). Furthermore, this inequality within homogeneous groups of workers has increased since 1970, which explains why the total inequality of the wage distribution (as measured, say, by the P90/P10 ratio) has been increasing steadily in the United States since 1970 (as discussed in Chapter 1), even though the return to education decreased during the 1970s. Similarly, although it is true that unemployment and underemployment affected less-skilled workers more than highly skilled ones, employment-related inequality increased among workers of similar skill levels, including the highly skilled. The theory of skill-biased technological change also implies that unemployment should have been greater among less-skilled workers in countries where wage inequality did not increase much, such as France, than in countries where increasing disparities of productivity were compensated by wage differences, such as the United States. But while it is true that the unemployment rate among less-skilled workers is much higher in France than in the United States, the unemployment rate of more-skilled workers is also higher by roughly the same proportion (Card et al., 1996).

Of course, one shouldn't underestimate the extreme inadequacy of wage surveys when it comes to reporting the individual characteristics on which economists rely as objective measures of individual skills. The significance of the available indicators varies so widely between countries that any international comparison based on such data is extremely hazardous: for example, in 1990, less than 25 percent of the active French population had a *baccalauréat* or higher degree, whereas more than 85 percent of the active US population had a high school diploma or higher (Lefranc, 1997, fig. 1), so that the group described as "unskilled" in the United States was much narrower than the comparable group in France. Reality clearly contains many more shades of difference than our mediocre sources suggest: the uneven quality of American high schools is well known.

The poor quality of available data is also a problem when it comes to studying the evolution of wage inequality within a particular country. For example, the data generally include only the total number of years of study and not the level of the university or the type of degree a worker holds. But every employer has access to this type of information when hiring and can differentiate between different levels of education despite the equivalence in number of years, which is the only information available to the economist. Furthermore, the type of diploma a person holds may also be used as a "signal" of qualities other than education-related skills (Spence, 1974). If so, the fact that we can only observe the number of years of study makes it impossible to measure what really matters to employers. This is one of the traditional limitations of using observable individual characteristics to explain wage inequality: a considerable portion of overall inequality remains unexplained. It is plausible to assume that within groups sharing the same observable characteristics, actual human capital inequality increased after 1970. For instance, two different degrees requiring the same number of years of study might equip the student with very different skills.

Proponents of the theory of skill-biased technological change thus rely on very flexible definitions of human capital. The risk is that the theory then becomes completely tautological: it is always possible to "explain" any observed wage distribution by invoking corresponding productivity differences supposedly stemming from unobservable individual characteristics. Although this theory surely explains a significant part of the increase in wage inequality and inequality with respect to employment, to expect it to explain all the observed data given the current state of knowledge would be unreasonably optimistic.

Wage Inequality and Globalization

Human capital theory has also been used to explain rising wage inequality resulting from globalization. The rise of North-South trade has allegedly put less-skilled workers in the North in competition with cheap labor in the South, consequently reducing their compensation and increasing wage inequality. Although logically plausible, this explanation encounters a major obstacle: although imports from the Third World have significantly increased since 1970, they accounted for only 2–2.5 percent of Western GDP in 1990, or barely 10 percent of the developed countries' international trade (Freeman, 1995, p. 16). How can such a small percentage of all goods and services produced in the West be responsible for such a broad increase in wage inequality? It is logically possible, of course, that supply and demand for different skill levels cause rising inequality in a few sectors affected by international trade to diffuse to the rest of the economy, but this hypothesis needs to be verified empirically. Furthermore, it has been shown that in the United States and United Kingdom, the segregation of workers with different human capital endowments in different firms, as measured by the correlation of wages among employees of the same firm, increased significantly in all sectors of the economy and not only in sectors affected by international trade (Kremer and Maskin, 1996). The same kind of segregation has been observed in France (Kramarz et al., 1995), suggesting a growing divide between different production units, some being ultraproductive while others produce far less efficiently. In the current state of knowledge, these findings seem to indicate that the growth of wage inequality stems from internal structural changes in the production process within the developed countries and that similar changes would have occurred if those countries had been closed economies not trading with the rest of the world.

How to Redistribute Labor Income

Suppose that wage inequality is in fact explained by inequality of human capital. What would the implications be for redistribution? Assume, further, that it is impossible, at least in the short run, to influence human capital inequality itself, so that the only thing that can be done is to redistribute incomes spontaneously determined by the market. This would be a pure redistribution, justified by considerations of social justice alone: human capital inequality is at least partly a result of factors beyond the control of individuals, such as social background, natural talent, and unequal initial endowments. Under such circumstances, what is the best way to redistribute?

As in the case of capital/labor redistribution (discussed in Chapter 2), the key question is whether substitution between different types of human capital is possible at the level of the economy as a whole. If the economy is constrained to use fixed proportions of different types of labor (*n* workers per computer specialist, say), so that the total number of employees of each type is fixed, then direct redistribution, to be achieved by, say, setting a high minimum wage and a low maximum wage, is completely equivalent to fiscal redistribution, in which the market is allowed to set wages but high earners are taxed to finance transfer payments to low earners (or to reduce their taxes). If there is substantial elasticity of substitution between different types of labor (defined in the same way we defined elasticity of capital/labor substitution in Chapter 2), however, fiscal redistribution is strictly superior: it allows increasing the income of relatively unskilled workers by the same proportion as direct redistribution but without increasing the cost of low-skilled labor to the firm and thus without decreasing the number of low-skilled jobs. Once again, the superiority of fiscal redistribution comes from the fact that, unlike direct redistribution, it severs the connection between the price paid by the firm and the price received by the worker. This argument is quite general and does not apply only to redistribution between workers of different skill levels. For example, a system of family allocations financed by a deduction from workers' paychecks would make it possible to redistribute wages to workers with children without increasing their cost to firms, in contrast to a direct distribution asking employers to pay a higher wage to workers with children than to those without.

Again, empirical studies confirm the existence of such substitutability: demand for low-skilled labor decreases relative to demand for skilled labor when its relative cost rises, and vice versa. All available econometric studies show that the elasticities in question are systematically higher than the elasticity of capital/labor substitution (Krussel et al., 1996; Hamermesh, 1986) (compare Chapter 2), and these findings are confirmed by historical work on major structural shifts in employment in various countries and periods. It is easier to replace low-skilled workers with machinery or skilled workers than to do without skilled workers.

However, the superiority of fiscal transfers and allocation by price is no more readily accepted in regard to wage redistribution than in regard to capital/labor redistribution. The left remains skeptical about reducing employer-paid social charges on low-wage workers. The idea that the payment of unequal wages—possibly quite unequal wages—to different categories of workers might play a useful allocative role is hard to accept, as is the idea that wages should therefore be allowed to adjust freely, while using taxes and transfers to correct the resulting unjust distribution of income. If wage inequality is unjust, the skeptics argue, why not simply require firms to pay less unequal wages? The problem here is the same as the one we discussed earlier in relation to capital/labor redistribution: in a complex world where many different goods and services are produced, a high price for skilled relative to less-skilled labor may not be the worst way to encourage firms and consumers to choose goods and services that make intensive use of less-skilled labor and less-intensive use of high-skilled labor. Fiscal redistribution makes it possible to preserve the allocative role of the price system while redistributing income between workers.

A Major Political Issue

As in the case of capital/labor substitution, the political stakes are considerable: if the rise of wage inequality since 1970 is due to skill-biased technological change and growing disparities in individual productivity, then the only way to create jobs is to ensure that prices paid by firms and consumers for different types of labor vary in the same proportions. The P90/P10 wage ratio in the United States in the 1990s is 4.5, whereas it is "only" 3.2 in France (Table 1.7). From this one might deduce that in order to create as many jobs in France as in the United States, and in particular in order to stop the labor share of value added from decreasing further in France, one ought to increase the C90/C10 ratio between the 90th and 10th percentiles of wages plus social charges in France by about 40 percent, which would mean eliminating all employer-paid social charges on low wages and reassigning them to high wages. This solution (using social charges to change the C90/C10 ratio rather than seeking to increase the P90/P10 ratio of wages actually received by workers) is preferable by far: not only is it more just, since low-wage workers, who are already disadvantaged, should not be expected to pay the price of skill-biased technological change; it is also the only solution that avoids the withdrawal of the least-skilled portion of the work force from the labor market, as seen in the United States (compare Chapter 1).

In fact, all French governments since 1978 have tried to do just this: social charges, which were previously capped and therefore less of a burden on high earners than on low earners, were gradually uncapped in 1978–1979 and 1982–1984 for medical charges and in 1989–1990 for family charges, and then the charges were reduced for low-wage workers in 1993. This increased the C90/C10 ratio above the P90/P10 ratio in 1993: the C90/C10 fell from 3.4 in 1970 to 2.9 in 1983 during the "great compression" of wages in France, before rising to 3.4 in 1995, while the P90/P10 ratio remained constant (INSEE, 1996a, p. 51). This put France at the level of the United States in the early 1970s, before wage inequality began to increase (Table 1.7). It is therefore tempting to conclude that France still has a long way to go to reach the 4.5 ratio that exists in the United States, and that more must be done to shift social charges from low to high earners (see Chapter 4).

These comparisons should be viewed cautiously, however. For example, the P90/P10 wage ratio in the United Kingdom was 3.3 at the beginning of the 1990s (Table 1.7), and the C90/C10 ratio was slightly higher owing to the reduction of social charges on low earners, and this did not prevent British firms and consumers from choosing more labor-intensive goods and services, whereas the wage share of output continued to fall in France. Of course, the United Kingdom remains poorer than France, with a lower average wage, so it may be benefiting from a certain amount of catch-up as per the convergence model.

Where Does Human Capital Inequality Come From?

Fiscal redistribution makes it possible to limit the effects of human capital inequality on standards of living without doing anything about the structural causes of inequality. The cause of human capital inequality remains a central question. If, moreover, Gary Becker and his Chicago colleagues are staunchly in favor of the free market, it is not so much because they believe that human capital inequality is the primary cause of wage inequality as because of their theory of the origins of human capital inequality itself. For Becker and his colleagues, the acquisition of human capital is much like any other investment: if the cost of the investment (the price of education, length of study, and so on) is lower than the "return" on that investment (the additional income available thanks to the increment of human capital), then the market will find the necessary funds to finance the profitable investment, just as the market model predicts for investments in physical capital with perfect credit markets. Similarly, if the experience and on-the-job training afforded by a certain job yield a significant increment of human capital, then the worker who is free to choose will accept a lower wage or even pay the employer to have the job in order to acquire the additional capital.

If this theory is correct, two consequences follow immediately, and it is worth distinguishing between them. First, the cost of substantial fiscal redistribution of wages would be considerable, because it would decrease the return on investments in human capital and thus decrease the incentive for individuals to make such investments, thereby reducing the number of high-wage jobs to such a degree that low-wage jobs would also suffer. In other words, if doctors were not allowed to earn ten times as much as workers to compensate them for their long years of study, there would be fewer doctors to care for the workers and pay taxes. The theory of human capital investments thus holds that the elasticity of the supply of human capital (defined in an analogous way to the elasticity of the supply of capital) is very high. A second, subsidiary argument is sometimes made as well: it is not only counterproductive but also unjust to redistribute wages because different individual investments in human capital reflect different preferences in regard to length of study, arduousness of work, and so on, and the government has no business judging these different preferences. In practice, however, the most common argument is that the elasticity of the supply of human capital is high. But how true is it that wage redistribution runs up against a problem of incentives? Unfortunately, empirical estimates are much harder to come by than theoretical treatises in this area. Nevertheless, in the current state of our knowledge, it is fair to say that the elasticity effects are much smaller than the Chicago theorists imagine (see Chapter 4).

Efficient Inequality?

The second consequence of the theory of efficient investment in human capital is that it is pointless for the state to intervene to reduce human capital inequality. Because the free play of market forces and private initiative is supposed to ensure that all profitable investments in education and training have already been made, any intervention in the education or labor markets can only do harm. In other words, the theory implies not only that pure redistribution creates a problem of incentives and must therefore be limited in scope but also that no efficient redistribution is possible, because the market allocation of resources is already optimally efficient (in Pareto's sense, as discussed in the Introduction).

These recommendations may at first sight seem surprising to anyone accustomed to reasoning in terms of the ways in which inequality of educational opportunity is reproduced from generation to generation. One justification for government intervention in the educational arena is simply that the young students at whom interventionist policies are directed are generally incapable of judging the profitability of any particular educational investment, and their parents are not necessarily much better equipped to do so. Although economists hesitate to invoke such "paternalistic" arguments, it is hard to deny that if the children of India were to follow the advice of the Chicago theorists and wait until market forces and parental initiative conspired to teach them to read, India would very likely remain mired in misery for a long time to come. Compulsory elementary education is no doubt the most important of all instruments for efficient redistribution, and research on growth and convergence suggests that the considerable improvements in standards of living achieved in the West since the nineteenth century would not have been possible without such schooling.

Another argument against the theory of efficient human capital investments is of course the imperfection of the credit market, on which I touched earlier. This may prevent individuals from poorer families from undertaking long courses of study even if they have the ability to make the investment profitable. The market failure is compounded by the fact that investments in human capital are long term, but since it is difficult to make a credible commitment to repay an educational loan, loans are granted more readily to students whose parents can offer guarantees. On these grounds one can justify generous financial support to students from modest backgrounds as a remedy for the inefficiently inegalitarian distribution of human capital endowments.

There are, however, no reliable empirical estimates of the quantitative importance of this type of credit market failure, and the paternalistic argument does not apply equally to education at all levels. To be sure, educational achievement varies strongly with social origin, and children from modest backgrounds generally pursue their studies for a shorter time than those from wealthier backgrounds with similar test scores at age ten. It is tempting to conclude that these students would have continued their studies longer in the absence of imperfect credit markets. But some sociologists suggest that the finding can also be explained by the hypothesis that students from modest backgrounds are less motivated to pursue lengthy courses of study because they are not expected to maintain the same family standing (Boudon, 1973).

This is the sociological version of the "different preferences" argument. It implies that it is misleading to think that inequality of opportunity could be reduced substantially by increasing public investment in the education of students from modest backgrounds. In fact, the influence of social origin on professional success goes well beyond the problems of credit market failure and access to education: controlling for the level of educational attainment, the effects of social origin are statistically significant at every career stage (Goux and Maurin, 1996). More generally, the fact that level of education explains only a part of overall wage inequality is often invoked to temper the enthusiasm of those who think they can end inequality by enacting ambitious educational reforms (Boudon, 1973). If paying for studies were the key explanatory factor, moreover, one would expect to find a higher level of intergenerational reproduction of human capital in countries such as the United States, where private financing of education plays an essential role, than in Europe, where public financing is predominant. In fact, it seems that intergenerational mobility with respect to level of education does not vary much at all across time and space (Shavit and Blossfeld, 1993), nor does intergenerational mobility with respect to level of income (Erikson and Goldthorpe, 1992).

The Role of the Family and Educational Expenses

Broadly speaking, skeptics of state intervention in education do not deny the importance of the family in reproducing inequality of human capital but rather seek to show that inequality inevitably persists because of the family's central role. Becker's theories of the family, as presented in his own works and those of his students (Becker, 1991; Mulligan, 1996), emphasize the choices that families make when investing in their children in order to show that any state intervention would risk undermining them. This is an old intellectual tradition in Chicago. In 1966, the sociologist James Coleman produced a famous report for the US government on the education of disadvantaged minorities. The report caused a scandal because it argued that the redistribution of financial resources to schools in disadvantaged neighborhoods had not yielded any noticeable improvement in educational outcomes or success in the job market. The Coleman Report and other work in the same vein concluded that simply spending more money on education in disadvantaged communities will not improve outcomes because it is within the family unit and the immediate social environment that inequality inevitably originates.

Of course, everyone agrees that the factors influencing the transmission of inequality are far more "environmental" than genetic. Or almost everyone: the psychologist Richard Herrnstein and the sociologist Charles Murray made front-page news in 1994 when they published *The Bell Curve,* which many critics accused of defending the idea that intelligence is to a large extent genetically determined. In fact, Herrnstein and Murray also recognized that adoption studies showed that children from disadvantaged sociocultural backgrounds placed at birth in more highly educated families were just as successful as the biological offspring of those families (Herrnstein and Murray, 1994, pp. 410–413). But this is not really the central issue. If the key factors have to do with the family environment, and in particular with the family environment in early childhood (books in the home, conversations with parents, etc.), so that nothing can really alter inequality established within the home at this stage of life, then the consequences are not very different from those of genetically determined inequality. Thirty years after Coleman, Herrnstein and Murray also stressed the idea that because it is difficult to detect the effects of investing educational resources in disadvantaged communities, it is pointless to persist with such policies.

If this theory were valid, there would be no reason to try to alter the unequal distribution of human capital. It would be better to spend the available funds to reduce unequal living standards by means of fiscal transfers, within the (potentially strict) limits defined by the elasticity of the supply of human capital.

The Problem of Inefficient Segregation of Human Capital

These claims stimulated a great deal of debate, especially in the United States after the Coleman Report was published. More recent work, using better indicators of the effects of additional spending on education in disadvantaged neighborhoods, shows that the earlier claims were greatly overstated (Card and Krueger, 1992). Moreover, Coleman's findings can be interpreted in different ways. In fact, it is plausible to think that the effects of educational spending are small not because the family environment is the sole determinant of scholastic success but because the effects of the school and neighborhood social environment are greater than those of educational spending per se.

In other words, it is plausible to think that a student's chance of scholastic success depends more on the "quality" of his classmates than on that of his teacher, especially at the primary and secondary level. It is unlikely that scholastic success can be improved significantly by sending a highly trained teacher into a difficult inner-city neighborhood, but sending students from that same neighborhood to a highly rated high school or prep school is much more likely to increase their probability of success. This hypothesis has been confirmed with the help of a very rich set of intergenerational data from the United States, the Panel Study of Income Dynamics (PSID), which shows that for a given level of parental education and income, the likelihood of upward social mobility for the children varies over a range of two to one depending on the average income of the neighborhood in which the parents live. These results show that "local externalities," which economists have long measured at the microeconomic level of the classroom, can have a substantial effect on the global dynamics of inequality—of the same order of magnitude as the effect of parental characteristics themselves (Cooper et al., 1994).

Thus, negative results such as Coleman's, rather than bolstering the opposition to state intervention to redistribute financial resources to disadvantaged neighborhoods, suggest a need for more radical redistributive methods, such as redrawing school zones to require parents from different groups to send their children to the same schools (given the impossibility of requiring them to live in the same neighborhoods). Such policies exist in many countries, but generally on a very small scale: parental choice is often limited in order to avoid too much social imbalance in the classroom, but geographical limitations on school rezoning significantly curtail the attainable level of social mixing. More radical policies such as busing were tried briefly in a number of US cities in the 1960s and 1970s, generally in order to achieve better racial mixing. School busing marked the culmination of the civil rights era in the United States, but the policy met with significant parental hostility. This should not have come as a surprise in the United States, where parents have long been accustomed to local control of schools, including curricula and teacher hiring.

Nevertheless, parental decisions about where to send children to school have major consequences on other children, and the anonymity of the price system (in this case, the price of housing) prevents parents from taking into account the externalities that their choices imply for others. Thus, even where social integration would have benefited disadvantaged youngsters far more than it would have cost advantaged ones, researchers have shown how individual housing choices nevertheless resulted in segregation (Benabou, 1993). In theory, it is therefore possible that everyone would benefit from social integration (for example, if the costs of integration for advantaged groups are less than the tax savings resulting from the scholastic and professional success of the disadvantaged), but such a social equilibrium cannot be achieved without collective coercion. Simple rules (such as requiring that average parental income be equal in all schools in a given community) might therefore be in everyone's best interest in the long run.

Discrimination in the Labor Market

Another socioeconomic mechanism leading to inefficient human capital inequality is labor market discrimination. Initially developed by Phelps (1968) and Arrow (1973) to explain discrimination against African Americans in the United States, the theory of labor market discrimination can also be applied to any other group in which employers are able to observe distinguishing characteristics of group members: women, lower castes in India, the long-term unemployed, or, more generally, any group whose members are subject to negative prejudices. The basic idea is simple. Suppose that employers predict that certain social groups are objectively less likely than others to contain members with sufficient human capital to qualify for certain jobs. Suppose, further, that employers cannot observe the qualifications and motivations of each candidate with perfect accuracy at the time of hiring, so that hiring decisions are made on the basis of imperfect signals, such as the results of a test, an interview, or a CV. Since the employers expect that certain groups are less likely to possess the required human capital, they will hire members of those groups only if their test results, say, are exceptionally good. In other words, the bar is set higher than for other groups. How will the groups subject to such discrimination react to this practice on the part of employers? Since the probability of being hired for a skilled job is low, members of such groups will be less likely on average to make the necessary investments in human capital and will do so only if they believe they are likely to perform exceptionally well on the hiring test or interview. For example, only those with high confidence in their abilities will undertake long courses of study, prepare intensively for job interviews, and so on. In other words, their behavior will tend to validate the expectations of the employers, namely, that the average level of human capital in the group subject to discrimination is in fact lower than in other groups. It can then be shown that even if the two groups (people of color and whites, say) are equally capable of acquiring the necessary human capital, and *a fortiori* if one of the groups is initially slightly less capable because its members come from more modest social backgrounds, the employers' expectations will influence the behavior of group members in a perverse way to produce a deep and persistent inequality of human capital and professional achievement (Coate and Loury, 1993).

This human capital inequality is totally inefficient because it is based entirely on a self-fulfilling prophecy. Economic efficiency requires that groups with identical capabilities make identical investments in human capital. Inequality due to discrimination is therefore profoundly perverse. This economic theory of discrimination is similar in some ways to sociological theories that hold that inequality is often the result of a dominant discourse that becomes a self-fulfilling prophecy: if it is widely believed that the members of certain groups are unlikely to succeed, they will be discouraged from trying (Bourdieu and Passeron, 1964; 1970).

Affirmative Action versus Fiscal Transfers

The political implications of these theories are important. If a significant part of inequality is in fact due to perverse mechanisms of the sort described, then new redistributive instruments are needed. For example, the theory of discrimination suggests that employers should be prohibited by law from discriminating against minorities. One way to do this is to require employers to show that each hiring and promotion decision is based on unbiased objective criteria. Another is to impose affirmative action quotas, requiring employers to hire a certain percentage of minority workers, in order to break the vicious circle of self-fulfilling prophecies of failure. Such affirmative action policies became popular in the United States in the 1970s to protect African Americans, women, and other minorities. Affirmative action, which in some ways resembles earlier efforts to use labor law to limit employer discretion in hiring and promotion, is very different from the kinds of policies recommended by human capital theorists, who say that the best remedy for inequality is to make fiscal transfers to social groups whose human capital endowments are too low (within the limits imposed by the elasticity of the supply of human capital), while of course avoiding any interference in the process of production. Herrnstein and Murray (1994) challenge the very idea of discrimination and argue that racial inequality persists because low IQ and low levels of human capital are transmitted from generation to generation within African-American families.

Can this controversy be settled with data? In the relatively well-documented case of African Americans in the United States, the observed facts appear to support the theory of discrimination. Freeman (1973) shows that the only way to explain the reduction of the wage gap between African Americans and whites after the civil rights movement of the 1960s is to invoke the progressive erosion of negative prejudices against African Americans and the discouragement that resulted from such prejudices (see also Bound and Freeman, 1989). But the best example is surely the impressive improvement in the situation of women in the labor market since 1950, which can only be explained by appeal to a theory insisting on the importance of discrimination, prejudice, and discourse in the production of inequality. In all Western countries, the participation of women in the labor market rose from a mere 10–20 percent in 1950 to more than 50 percent in the 1980s (OECD, 1985). Progress continued in the 1980s and 1990s: while wages increased across the board, the average woman's wage in the United States rose more than 20 percent relative to the average man's (Blau and Kahn, 1994). The same was true in most other developed countries (OECD, 1993, pp. 176–178). No fiscal transfer could have brought about such a spectacular improvement in the economic situation of women.

Furthermore, this improvement also occurred in countries with "Mediterranean" (pro-natalist) tax systems (such as the family quotient in France), which discourage women's participation in the labor force, compared with the United States, United Kingdom, and Scandinavian countries, where individuals are taxed rather than households.* In short, inequalities based on rank discrimination, such as between people of color and whites or men and women, are much more susceptible to remedy by affirmative action and changes in mentality than by any kind of fiscal redistribution.

Unfortunately, the fact that an inequality is based on discrimination does not always mean that it is easy to eliminate or even reduce. For example, most observers agree that the results of affirmative action in the United States have been mixed at best. Indeed, quotas requiring employers to hire a certain percentage of people of color can reinforce rather than weaken prejudices against African Americans, "who become employable only when we are forced to employ them," while at the same time reducing their incentive to compete for jobs like other citizens, which is precisely the opposite of the intended goal (Coate and Loury, 1993). Many observers therefore denounce the quota system. The apparent ineffectiveness of affirmative action contributed greatly to the conservative reaction against social programs in general in the 1980s and 1990s. In fact, it is likely that the deterioration of the relative position of African Americans in the labor market since the 1970s, which fueled this reaction, is more simply explained as a by-product of the general increase in wage inequality and of deindustrialization, which hit African American workers hard, especially in the northern United States (Wilson, 1987).

The Social Determination of Wage Inequality

Some wage inequalities cannot be explained solely in terms of an underlying inequality of human capital (whether efficient or inefficient). For example, certain economic actors (such as firms or trade unions) may attempt to manipulate the wage structure resulting from

---

* The family quotient results in a tax abatement for large families.—Trans.

the supply and demand of human capital to their advantage. Other considerations, such as the need to motivate workers, may lead employers to look to factors other than human capital. Even in the absence of overt manipulation of market prices for labor, this can distort the wage structure in ways not predicted by the theory of human capital. Are these deviations from competitive prices a good thing or a bad thing? How does the existence of such deviations affect the question of redistributing labor income?

The Role of Unions in Setting Wages

What do unions do? The traditional economic analysis is simple: unions exercise monopoly power in the wage-setting process. The legal rights they are granted entitle them to represent the interests of large numbers of workers, and no worker can offer to work for a lower wage than that to which the union agrees. Just as a firm with monopoly power will choose to raise prices even if it means losing a few customers, a union will use its monopoly power to demand wages higher than would otherwise prevail, even if it means lowering the overall level of employment. This analysis neglects the fact that unions generally fight not just for higher wages but also for a certain compression of the wage hierarchy within each firm. They achieve this second goal by insisting on wage schedules that limit the difference between the wages paid for different levels of experience and skill (Freeman and Medoff, 1984).

In any case, the tools that unions use to increase total labor income and decrease inequality between workers are not tools of efficient redistribution. As noted, wherever the possibility of capital/labor substitution and/or substitution of one type of labor for another exists at the level of the economy as a whole, any redistribution that involves manipulation of the price of labor and/or human capital is inefficient (Chapters 2 and 3). If labor unions are successful, firms will inevitably use more capital and less labor as well as more skilled labor and less unskilled labor. The fundamental fact is that it is always possible to

finance the same redistribution more efficiently by way of fiscal redistribution, that is, by taxing high earners to pay for fiscal transfers
to low earners, because this is the only way of severing the tie between
the price paid by the firm for labor and the amount received by the
worker. Hence the question is not how much redistribution from
capital to labor—and redistribution between workers—should exist,
because the answer to this question depends on other factors. It is
rather what instruments should be used for redistribution. Should
the wage-setting power of unions therefore be reduced?

Unions as Substitutes for Fiscal Redistribution?

The first response is that reducing the power of unions can make redistribution more efficient only if it actually results in replacing the
inefficient redistribution achieved by the unions with efficient fiscal
redistribution via the state. In practice, the problem is obviously that
there is no agreement about the proper extent of redistribution. Suppose that the current government decides that it is just for a low-skilled
employee to live on €760 a month while a highly skilled manager is
paid €4,575 a month. The government might reach such a decision because it believes that this is the only way to preserve the incentives
needed to encourage the manager to acquire the necessary skills. If a
union disagrees because it thinks that the employee should earn €1,525
a month and the manager only €3,810, then the only way to proceed
is to attempt to forcibly impose a new wage schedule on employers.
Of course, it would be better to increase the manager's tax by €760 a
month and use the proceeds to make a fiscal transfer of €760 to the
low-skilled worker. That way, the firm would not have to pay more to
its workers and less to its managers, which would inevitably lead to
hiring fewer workers and more managers and thus to an increase in
unemployment. But unions do not have the power to levy taxes and
make transfers. Historically, the role of unions has been to intervene
in conflicts of this type: when the state fails to play the redistributive
role that the unions believe it should play, they step in and use the re-

sources at their disposal: direct redistribution through struggle in the workplace.

These instruments are actually quite limited compared with fiscal redistribution. What is more, the results they achieve are often illusory. Once again we encounter the conflict between historical time and political time discussed in Chapter 2. As was the case with redistribution between capital and labor, fiscal redistribution has never substantially and visibly reduced labor income inequality between workers, although it has long been technically possible to do so. Historically, major fiscal redistributions have been rare and have generally taken the form of social expenditures rather than monetary transfers between workers (see Chapter 4). Even more important, they have always been put in place very gradually, so that their effects were felt only in the long run. Such reforms cannot fuel the political imagination on which social and political struggle thrive. Indeed, the long run may be so long that it makes no sense from the standpoint of any given generation.

By comparison, the inefficient redistributions achieved by direct manipulation of wages are much more visible. For example, the purchasing power of the minimum wage in France rose by about 92 percent between 1968 and 1983, a period in which trade unions played an essential role; during the same period, the average wage increased only 53 percent, which reduced the P90/P10 ratio from 4.2 in 1967 to 3.1 in 1983 (compare Chapter 1 and INSEE, 1996a, pp. 44, 48). By the same token, there is no denying that the two Western countries in which wage inequalities have increased most since the 1970s, namely, the United States and the United Kingdom, are also the two countries in which the power of unions has decreased most, in significant part due to political opposition.

Meanwhile, wage inequalities among employed workers have remained relatively stable in countries such as Germany and France, where the union coverage rate (that is, the percentage of workers covered by collective bargaining agreements) has remained relatively stable, even if the unionization rate (the percentage of workers belonging to unions) has decreased. This is a major reason for the contrasting evolution of wage inequalities in the West since the 1970s: it explains 20 to 40 percent of the observed variance (Card, 1992; Lemieux, 1993). This is totally overlooked by pure human capital theory and the theory of skill-biased technological change. It is possible that this union-driven redistribution has not been cost-free in terms of jobs created. But the fact remains that the United States and United Kingdom have not replaced inefficient union-driven redistribution by more efficient fiscal distribution; indeed, they have tended to reduce the latter as well. Under such conditions, unions can play a role as substitutes for fiscal redistribution.

Do Unions Contribute to Economic Efficiency?

The second response to the question of curtailing union power is that trade unions have at times served to promote economic efficiency. By representing workers, they facilitate better communication within the firm. Furthermore, the binding wage schedules negotiated by unions can under certain conditions be positive forces in themselves. For instance, human capital theory neglects the fact that a worker's skills and work habits are not necessarily qualities universally recognized by the market, which the worker can sell freely to whatever firm he chooses.

The value of specific forms of human capital is often unique to a particular firm, so that in practice the human capital market can never be fully competitive. Once a worker has made the necessary effort and investments to qualify for a specific job, the firm that hires him may pay a wage well below what his skills are worth, because the worker cannot make full use of his firm-specific skills in another firm. Anticipating this expropriation of his investment in human capital, the worker will not invest as fully as if he were certain of reaping the benefits for himself. Setting a floor wage below which the firm may not go can therefore resolve this problem and increase economic efficiency by ensuring that efficient investment opportunities are not neglected.

More generally, setting in advance the wage or wage range that a firm must pay to a worker with specific skills in a specific job category can provide an incentive for potential workers to acquire more firm-specific forms of human capital without fear of expropriation by the employer.

This type of phenomenon is not limited to the case of firm-specific human capital. A binding wage schedule is, in effect, a commitment not to expropriate, and this can also allow the firm itself to invest in its workers and reap the benefits. For example, foreign observers have long been astonished to discover that German firms finance costly training and apprenticeship centers. Apprentices are generally not re-quired to pay for the training or commit themselves to working for the firm even though much of the training they receive is of a general nature and could also be used in other firms. The most convincing ex-planation of this is that all firms in a given sector of industry agree to pay the same entry wage and standardized pay increments, thus en-suring that apprentices won't be lured away by competing firms after they are trained (Harhoff and Kane, 1994).

Characteristic features of the wage relation (such as firm-specific human capital and limited possibility of commitment) may therefore make efficient operation of the labor market dependent on certain types of collective regulation (such as binding wage schedules [Piketty, 1994, pp. 788–791]) and government interventions to correct market failures related to occupational training (Booth and Snower, 1996). In theory, then, the continued existence of binding wage schedules in some countries is not a costly and inefficient way of limiting the increase of wage inequality but potentially a means of encouraging new investments in human capital and thus limiting human capital in-equality in the future. Nevertheless, in the absence of additional empirical evidence, these arguments obviously cannot be used as systematic justification for centralized wage schedules. For example, there is no convincing evidence that the rigid wage schedules that have enabled certain Western countries to avoid rising wage inequality since the 1970s actually encouraged investments that would lead to more jobs and higher wages in the future.

The Monopsony Power of Employers

Although unions are often said to exercise monopoly power that enables them to raise wages about the competitive market level, economists are less likely to admit that employers sometimes exercise similar market power. Among noneconomists, however, the idea that employers exercise arbitrary power, to which workers respond by organizing unions, is commonplace. In the jargon of economics, the equivalent of the monopoly power of unions is the monopsony power of employers. A monopsony exists when there is only a single possible buyer for a given good, whereas a monopoly exists when there is only a single possible vendor. A monopolist can demand a price for his good above the competitive market price (at the risk of inducing customers to buy less of it), while a monopsonist can insist on paying less than the competitive market price for the good he wishes to buy (at the risk of inducing suppliers to sell less of it). The manipulation of market prices thus always decreases the quantity of goods exchanged, regardless of whether it is to the benefit of the buyer or seller. In the case of the labor market, a monopsonist employer will oblige his workers to accept a below-market wage, at the risk of discouraging some workers and thus diminishing the level of employment.

If monopsony exists, the redistributive implications are significant. For one thing, it would be inefficient to try to improve the workers' lot by means of fiscal transfers, because the employer would take advantage of the transfer to lower his wage offer. Efficient redistribution would then require an increase in the legal minimum wage in order to bring the wage paid by the firm closer to the competitive wage. This would also stimulate the supply of labor and thus increase the total employment level. In contrast to the usual conclusion, direct redistribution would then be superior to fiscal redistribution, because it would restore the competitive market equilibrium (after which fiscal transfers would be a more efficient means of further redistribution). For workers this would be the best of all possible worlds, since it would be possible both to improve their standard of living and reduce unemployment without spending a cent of tax revenue.

What might give employers monopsony power? Monopsony power can arise because of the existence of firm-specific human capital, which implies that workers are to some extent able to sell their labor to only one employer. More generally, limited geographical mobility or lack of information about other jobs may leave some workers at the mercy of a single employer. More simply, monopsony power can arise if a group of employers band together to impose a uniform wage schedule on their employees. Do such coalitions of capitalists actually exist? It is difficult to show empirically. In particular, it does not appear to be possible to explain increasing wage inequality in the United States since 1970 in this way. Indeed, the most striking thing about this phenomenon is that it occurred in an extremely competitive labor market. The compensation of lawyers, doctors, and managers has exploded since 1970, not because capitalists collectively decided to divide the labor market but because firms and individuals competed for their services, constantly hiring desired individuals away from their competitors by offering ever-increasing salaries. It does not follow that the ensuing inequality has to be accepted or even that the phenomenon itself is totally efficient. Nevertheless, the employer monopsony model cannot account for the observed facts.

When Does a Higher Minimum Wage Increase the Level of Employment?

Although monopsony cannot explain the global evolution of wage inequality, it is still possible for local monopsonies to exist, in particular in certain markets for unskilled labor with limited geographic mobility. In the 1990s, several studies of US labor markets, most notably Card and Krueger (1995), revived this debate. Using the fact that the legal minimum wage was raised at different dates by different amounts in various states in the 1980s and 1990s, economists convincingly demonstrated that the effect of an increase in the minimum wage on the employment level was generally positive and in any case fairly small. Note, in particular, a famous study of fast-food restaurants in New Jersey, where total employment rose after an increase in the state's minimum wage in 1992 (Card and Krueger, 1995, chap. 2). Larry Katz, the author of another of these studies, served as chief economist in the Department of Labor during the first Clinton administration, and this body of economic research surely influenced President Clinton's decision in 1996 to increase the federal minimum wage from $4.15 an hour to $5.20, or more than 20 percent, compared with a decline of more than 25 percent in the purchasing power of the federal minimum wage between 1980 and 1990.

The precise reasons why these minimum wage hikes had positive effects remain controversial, however. Was it the limited geographic mobility of low-wage workers that left them subject to a low-wage regime imposed by a local cartel of fast-food restaurants, so that the increase in the minimum wage did not decrease demand for their labor but instead increased supply by encouraging additional low-skilled youths to offer their services—thus exemplifying the theory of monopsony in its purest form? Or was it, as other studies suggest, that the increase in employment occurred because the higher minimum wage induced some young people to quit high school and replace less qualified workers (Neumark and Wascher, 1994)?

In any case, the fact remains that when the legal minimum wage falls as low as it did in the United States in the late 1980s and early 1990s, low-skilled jobs can become so unattractive that an increase in the minimum wage can increase the labor supply and the level of employment. More generally, the potential for local labor market (or firm-specific human capital) monopsonies is justification enough for a legal minimum wage in order to make sure that no employer can exploit a monopsony situation beyond a certain limit.

Efficiency Wages and Fair Wages

If there were no union monopolies, no employer monopsonies, no minimum wage, and no visible market failures, would the wages paid by firms for different types of labor be determined solely by supply and demand, as the theory of human capital suggests? The question might seem absurd, since every labor market we know has unions demanding the highest wage they think they can obtain for their members, employers seeking to pay workers as little as possible for their labor, and governments trying to arbitrate between the two and to achieve some measure of redistribution. A more useful question to ask is the following: Is the ability of labor unions to distort market prices a result of the legal rights they are granted (the right to strike, the closed shop, and so on), or would distorted prices continue to exist (to some extent, at least) without such rights?

Why would employers in a competitive labor market that prevents them from offering wages lower than those offered by their competitors choose to pay even higher wages? Because by increasing wages they obtain something of equal value from their workers. For example, suppose it is impossible for the employers to monitor the diligence of their workers. A higher wage might be intended to motivate workers to work harder, because the workers know they might lose something if sacked and forced to seek work with another employer, who doesn't pay such a high wage. Indeed, in sectors where it is difficult to monitor workers, we do observe wage differences that cannot be explained by differences in human capital (Krueger and Summers, 1988). This theory, which has often been invoked to explain unemployment in Europe in the period 1980–1990 (see, for example, Phelps, 1994), also implies that if all firms paid higher wages to motivate their workers, employment would decrease, so that what motivates workers is really the risk of a period of unemployment between jobs. Another version of this "efficiency wage" model assumes that in addition to potential loss of wages or risk of unemployment, workers may be more cooperative if they believe they are being paid a fair wage. It will then be in the firm's interest to pay something close to the perceived fair wage, even if it means decreasing overall employment (Akerlof and Yellen, 1990). Individual judgments of fairness are frequently quite important in the wage-setting process (Kahneman et al., 1986; Bewley, 1994). Unemployment can then be analyzed as the result of a distributional conflict, even in the absence of unions. The implications of these models for redistribution are obvious: fiscal redistribution should try to match what is perceived as fair in order to reduce the inefficiency of direct redistribution by reducing the charges on low earners and shifting them to high earners and/or corporate profits.

National Traditions and Wage Inequality

More generally, the theory of human capital, even when supplemented by manipulation of prices by unions or employers, is based on the idea that one can always measure the contribution of each type of skill to the production process, thus providing an objective, measurable basis for the return to human capital. As the discussions of discrimination and firm-specific human capital showed, however, reality is often more complicated. Measuring the productivity of different types of human capital is not always easy, and the variance in such measurements often reflects national differences.

For example, as Rothenberg (1996) has shown, wage inequality increases when workers believe that employers are highly likely to evaluate their productivity correctly, because those who score low accept their fate, while those who score high will threaten to quit as a tactic to pressure their employer for higher pay. Such a totally decentralized process may explain why the United States and United Kingdom, where "faith in capitalism" has strengthened since the 1970s, are also the countries where wage inequalities have increased most. In an apparent confirmation of this theory, there has been a veritable explosion in the compensation of top managers (Goolsbee, 1997; Feenberg and Poterba, 2000). But it is hard to believe that the actual productivity of these managers has suddenly increased by a corresponding amount.

Similarly, it is difficult to explain why France, with a P90/P10 ratio of 4.2 in 1967, was the most inegalitarian country in the Western world (in terms of wages) in the late 1960s and early 1970s without mentioning certain distinctive French attitudes toward inequality. It is probably not the case that human capital inequality was actually higher in France at that time than it was elsewhere. In 1976, the French government was outraged when an OECD report indicated that it was the most inegalitarian country in the West. In fact, France suffers from an extreme form of "republican elitism": the French tend to overestimate the actual difference in productivity between a top manager who has graduated from an elite school and an ordinary worker. Any difference in pay is justified by the fact that both had access to *l'école républicaine,* the supposedly egalitarian public educational system— perceived as egalitarian despite the fact that the state spends ten times as much on a graduate of the elite École Polytechnique as on an average student. The French belief in educational meritocracy is also reflected in the relative stability of pay differences after graduation, compared with a much higher degree of variability in Germany (Morrisson, 1996, p. 111). Although the German system is less inegalitarian, it is probably just as good at offering incentives.

To be sure, the observed variation between countries is quite small compared with historical differences of inequality, but it is more striking to contemporary observers. Although some of this variation can be explained by institutional differences between countries (for example, the German apprenticeship system versus lavish spending on elite education in France), it is often exaggerated by specific perceptions within each society. In part this is due to different national histories, which human capital theory cannot explain and fiscal redistribution can only superficially influence.

FOUR

Instruments of Redistribution

The two previous chapters have tried to show how important it is to understand the socioeconomic causes of inequality in order to know what instruments of redistribution are most appropriate. In this chapter I will continue to analyze the most important of these tools in the light of contemporary experience. As I have done throughout, I will continue to distinguish between pure and efficient redistribution.

Pure Redistribution

The primary tool for pure redistribution is fiscal redistribution, which makes it possible to correct inequality due to unequal initial endowments and market forces while preserving as much as possible of the allocative role of the price system. I will focus here on fiscal redistribution of labor income. In Chapter 2, I analyzed some of the specific problems associated with the redistribution of capital income, which is less important than labor income.

Average and Marginal Rates of Redistribution

To what extent do governments rely on fiscal redistribution today? In practice, modern fiscal redistribution depends on a variety of taxes (such as income tax, value-added tax, social charges), transfers (such as family allowances, unemployment insurance, guaranteed minimum income, and pensions), and expenses paid directly by the government (for health, education, and so on). An index often used to measure the extent of taxes and transfers in a given country is the total of all taxes as a percentage of GDP. For example, obligatory taxes amount to

30–35 percent of GDP in the United States and United Kingdom, 45–50 percent in Germany and France, and 60–70 percent in the Scandinavian countries. This is a poor measure, however, because it tells us nothing about how taxes, transfers, and expenditures are distributed. Furthermore, different accounting conventions in different countries make it difficult to compare these numbers. In Sweden and other Nordic countries, for example, pensions and other state-paid income is taxed like other income, and this increases the tax burden by nearly 10 percent of GDP in a totally artificial way. In France, this would be tantamount to financing a pension increase by increasing social charges on retirees, which obviously has no effect on actual redistribution.

The only way to measure fiscal redistribution correctly is to use the effective average and marginal rates of taxation and transfer. The effective average rate for a given level of income is defined as the sum of all taxes (or transfers) expressed as a percentage of gross income before taxes and transfers. The rate can be positive or negative, depending on whether the total tax paid is greater or smaller than the total transfers received. The effective marginal rate of tax and transfer between two income levels is defined as the sum of all taxes and transfers that an individual pays or receives if she transitions from one income level to another, expressed as a percentage of the difference in gross income. Effective marginal rates are generally positive, since an increase in gross income generally leads to an increase in taxes paid, but in principle it could also be negative if a higher income entitled a person to a higher transfer (or lower net tax).

These average and marginal rates are effective only to the extent that the numerator includes all taxes and transfers. In particular, it is essential to include all social charges, including those paid by employers. As we saw earlier, employer-paid social charges do not result in redistribution from capital to labor and in the end are always paid by labor (Chapter 2). Ideally, nonmonetary transfers achieved through government spending should also be included (I will return to this point). Figure 4.1 shows the average and effective marginal rates for different deciles of the wage distribution in France in 1996, taking account of income taxes, social charges, and social benefits (guaranteed minimum income, housing allowances, and so on) for single individuals (Piketty, 1997a).

The Absence of Redistribution between Workers

Figure 4.1 shows that effective average rates are positive for all wage levels: other than a very small housing allowance for those earning close to the minimum wage, a worker with no children receives no direct monetary transfer. The effective average rate is also positive for low-wage workers with children, because the family allowance received is always very much smaller than the tax paid, unless the number of children is very high. Last but not least, Figure 4.1 shows that effective rates do not vary much from one wage level to another: they are

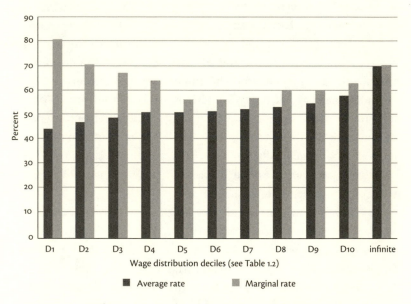

FIGURE 4.1. Effective marginal and average rates in France in 1996. Source: Piketty, 1997a.

on the order of 45 percent for the bottom two deciles of the wage distribution and on the order of 55 percent for the top two deciles, with the majority of average rates around 50 percent. The reason for this is simple: the proportionality of social charges largely outweighs the progressivity of the income tax. For example, in 1996, all workers, from minimum-wage employee to CEO, had to pay 6.8 percent of gross wages (approximately 8.5 percent of net) for health insurance. That 8.5 percent of net wages was about what a couple with one child earning F20,000 per month had to pay in income tax in 1996. The 6.8 percent health insurance charge represented barely 10 percent of total social charges, which amounted to roughly 65 percent of gross wages (20 percent paid by employees, 45 percent by employers).

This conclusion also holds for households with children: family allowances of course account for a higher percentage of supplementary income for low earners, but the family quotient system (which reduces the tax on large families) results in a larger decrease in income tax (as percentage of income) for high earners, so that the curve of average effective tax rates remains fairly flat. To be sure, as the "infinite income" bars in Figure 4.1 indicate, the effective average rate can go as high as 70 percent for very high earners who surpass all the ceilings for deductions and family quotients (applicable to those earning more than about F700,000 per year), who were liable to a top marginal income tax rate of 56.8 percent in 1996. But this affects very few households, so the actual importance of this top rate is much smaller than the symbolic importance often attached to it in political debate. In particular, it hardly alters the basic reality portrayed in Figure 4.1, namely, the absence of any substantial redistribution between workers. Including other proportional taxes such as the value-added tax, whose weight is twice that of the income tax, would further reinforce this conclusion.

These observations for France sum up the main feature of the contemporary fiscal redistribution in all Western countries, in spite of national institutional differences: there is no significant monetary redistribution between active workers. Taxation of active workers is broadly proportional and transfers are minimal, so that the variation in disposable income between active workers is quite close to the variation in wages paid by employers. As noted in Chapter 1, the countries in which income inequality is small are the countries in which wage inequality is low and vice versa. It is not the case that fiscal redistribution between workers reduces initially high wage inequalities. In addition to traditional expenditures (on justice, defense, highways, and so on), this broadly proportional tax essentially serves to pay for unemployment insurance, educational expenses, and above all pensions and health care. In some cases, these expenditures are advantageous to workers at the low end of the wage scale, but this is not always the case. I will say more about this later.

The U-Shaped Curve of Marginal Rates

Effective average rates of tax and transfer can measure the degree of redistribution that actually occurs, but to measure the impact of this redistribution on individual behavior, effective marginal rates are more useful. Figure 4.1 shows that effective marginal rates are higher at both the low end and the high end of the income distribution than in the middle, creating a rather marked U-shaped curve. It is not surprising that marginal rates are higher at the top end: high earners are in the top income-tax brackets. Marginal rates are also higher at the low end because a person who goes from zero wage income to some wage income must not only pay taxes on his pay but also lose certain social transfer payments available only to those who have no income from work. Consider, for example, an unemployed person in France who receives €530 per month in guaranteed basic income and housing allotment but who then finds an employer prepared to pay €1,370 a month for his labor, presumably because his contribution to the production process brings in at least that amount. The worker will actually receive just over €760 in net income each month after deducting all social charges. In other words, his gross income goes from 0 to 1,370, but his disposable income goes from 530 to 760. The worker's additional income is just €230 per month, or less than 20 percent, which yields an effective marginal tax rate of more than 80 percent, as shown in Figure 4.1 for the first decile of the wage distribution. If the worker has children or was entitled to unemployment benefits before finding work, the calculation would be slightly different, but the effective marginal rate would still be on the order of 80–90 percent, and in some cases more than 100 percent (for details, see Piketty, 1997a).

As it turns out, low-wage workers bear the highest effective marginal rates: a single worker moving from the ninth to the tenth decile of the wage distribution faces a maximum marginal rate on the order of 60 percent and 70 percent for an infinite income in the top income tax bracket (assuming no special deductions), compared with a rate on the order of 80–90 percent for a person moving from unemployment into the first decile of the wage distribution. This U-shaped curve of effective marginal rates, with the highest peaks at the bottom end of the curve, is the second major characteristic of contemporary fiscal redistribution. Once again, it is a characteristic shared by all Western countries: reserving social transfers for those who have no income from labor while excluding low-wage workers is, in appearance at any rate, the least costly way to fight poverty. It was this thinking that prevailed when national welfare systems were put in place.

Just Fiscal Redistribution

Are these curves of marginal and average effective rates of redistribution optimal from the standpoint of social justice? Should they be raised or lowered for different income groups?

The answers to these questions depend to a large extent on the magnitude of the negative effects that high redistribution rates may have on incentives to work and to supply human capital and therefore on redistribution itself. There is a fairly broad consensus concerning the fundamental purposes of pure redistribution: a redistribution is just if it does as much as possible to improve the opportunities and living standards of the least well off. This is John Rawls's maximin principle, discussed in the Introduction. Of course, controversy remains as to which individuals are the least well off. Since individuals differ in multiple dimensions, this is not always easy to decide, and this difficulty can pose problems when it comes to defining the idea of responsibility and setting the goals of social justice, as recent work in social justice theory has shown (Fleurbaey, 1996; Roemer, 1996).

The pragmatic conception of social justice expressed by the maximin principle—namely, that inequality is tolerable as long as any further redistribution would not be in the interest of the least well off—has also aroused objections of principle. Some critics reject the idea that the price system and individual self-interest form a sound basis for organizing an economy. Surveys show, however, that most people agree that inequalities due to factors beyond the control of individuals should be corrected insofar as it is possible to do so. The consensus on this point is even more striking when compared to the deep agreement that exists as to actions that are within the power of individuals and therefore the ways in which redistribution may alter incentives to behave in certain ways (Piketty, 1995). I turn to this conflict next. What is the practical effect of redistribution on incentives?

Do High Taxes Diminish Revenue?

In the 1980s, an idea gained popularity in the United States: high taxes are a disincentive to work by high achievers, so much so that tax revenues actually decline when rates are raised too much, so that high tax rates benefit no one. More broadly, all Western countries began to wonder whether their redistributive systems had attained their limits. Taxes, which had risen rapidly in previous decades, began to level off. These changes were most visible in the United States, where the top marginal income tax rate was progressively reduced from 70 percent in the late 1970s to 28 percent in 1986.

Traditional estimates of the elasticity of the supply of labor generally found that it was quite low, however, on the order of 0.1–0.2 percent (Blundell, 1995, p. 60). Of course, these studies measured the elasticity of the supply of labor and not of human capital as such. They considered only the effect of tax rates on the number of hours worked, which do not vary much for the majority of workers, and not on motivation or efficiency, nor on incentives to acquire additional human capital or find a more remunerative job, which are potentially more important. It is hard to imagine that these incentives are completely insignificant, even if they are difficult to measure. For example, the proportion of each age cohort entering higher education in the United States decreased by 5 percent from 1975 to 1980, while the return to a college degree decreased by 15 percent. Subsequently, the percentage pursuing higher education rose by about 10 percent in the 1980s (Ehrenberg and Smith, 1994, p. 289). These facts do not allow us to make a rigorous estimate of the elasticity of the supply of human capital, however, although they do suggest that the supply will eventually decrease if appropriate employment opportunities disappear.

One study of high incomes conducted after the 1986 tax reform in the United States concluded that the cut in top marginal rates had a significant incentive effect, with an elasticity on the order of 1 (Feldstein, 1995). This estimate applied only to very high earners, however. In addition, it seems that the bulk of the measured effect was owing to a transfer of earnings previously taxed as corporate income to earnings taxed as personal income rather than to actual new earnings due to incentives to work harder and acquire more human capital (Slemrod, 1995). Such transfers between different categories of income are common at the top end of the distribution, which therefore needs to be approached very cautiously. The top marginal income tax rate in the United States was gradually increased from 28 percent in 1986 to 39 percent in 1993, but this had no clear effect on the rate of growth of high incomes after 1993 (Goolsbee, 1997). French data appear to confirm Goolsbee's results. The ceiling placed on the family quotient in 1981 amounted to a sharp increase in the marginal tax rate on high-income households, while the marginal rate on unmarried individuals and childless couples remained unchanged. This made for a particularly interesting "natural experiment." A meticulous examination of the tax data shows that top earners in both groups increased their income at roughly the same rate, independent of the family quotient and therefore of differences in their marginal tax rates (Piketty, 1999).

Given the current state of our knowledge, the fact that marginal rates are higher at the lower end of the wage distribution than in the middle or at the top (Figure 4.1) suggests that too much attention has been paid to the supposed disincentive effects of higher top marginal rates. This has not been helpful for judging whether the modern welfare state has reached the limit of possible redistribution. In many countries estimates have been made of the effects of high marginal rates on labor market participation by initially unemployed individuals in various categories (youths, single people, and married women). All these studies have found much higher elasticities (ranging from 0.7 to 1.2) for these groups than for those already employed (Blundell, 1995, p. 59; for a study of recent French data, compare Piketty, 1998). In other words, the prospect of earning a decent living seems to be more of an incentive for low-income people than the prospect of a still-higher income for those who are already well off: "poverty traps" are likely to be more important than "middle-income traps." The evolution of the Earned Income Tax Credit (EITC) in the United States since the early 1990s has done much to invigorate this debate.

The Earned Income Tax Credit in the United States

The EITC, first introduced in 1975, is a tax credit that benefits people at the low end of the wage spectrum. Since its modest beginnings, it has blossomed into a central element of the American tax and welfare system. In 1996 the EITC offered a tax credit of 40 percent of earned income on incomes below $9,000 a year, decreasing gradually to 20 percent on incomes up to $29,000 a year. In other words, a worker who earned $9,000 in 1996 received a tax credit of $3,600. This tax credit was "reimbursable," meaning that the taxpayer received a check equal to the difference between the credit and the amount of tax due, which at this level of income was always less than 10 percent, thus increasing net disposable income by more than 30 percent. With the increase in the federal minimum wage in 1996, this measure represented an effort by the US government to make low-paid work more attractive. The fact that the EITC rate was increased rather suddenly and that the full rate applied only to low-income people with at least two children made it possible to measure in fairly convincing fashion the considerable positive effects of the measure on the level of employment in the target population, revealing an elasticity slightly greater than 1 (Eissa and Liebman, 1996; Liebman, 1996).

Suppose that the disincentive effects of redistribution are in fact higher at the bottom end of the income distribution than at the top. Then the U-shaped curve of effective marginal rates traditionally used to focus redistribution on the poorest workers might not be the most effective strategy: by eliminating the initial portion of the U curve, that is, by decreasing charges on low incomes and transferring them to middle and high incomes, where elasticities are lower, one could finance larger transfer payments to those who cannot find jobs. This would make the system of redistribution more just by improving the situation of the least well off. The absence of any substantial fiscal redistribution between workers would then be equally bad for the jobless. The experience of the EITC in the United States suggests that a flattening of the initial portion of the U curve may be a more important priority than the remedy more frequently recommended by many politicians, namely, reducing marginal tax rates at the top of the distribution.

Fiscal Redistribution to Reduce Unemployment?

The EITC experience also raises the more general question of the role of fiscal redistribution in reducing unemployment. Could the positive effects of the EITC on unemployment be obtained in a country like

France? The fact that low wages have collapsed in the United States and not in France might suggest instead that making low-wage jobs more attractive and avoiding "poverty traps" are not really issues in France. But the presumed gap between low wages in France and the United States should not be overestimated. True, for the first time in American history, bottom-end wages in the United States have fallen in absolute terms since the 1970s, but they were initially higher than in France, so that after the US federal minimum wage increase in 1996, French and American minimum wages were actually quite comparable: on January 1, 1997, the French minimum wage was F38 an hour gross or about 29.7 net after deducting 21.8 percent in social charges, while the federal minimum wage in the United States was $5.20 an hour (or $4.81 net after deduction of 7.5 percent). At an exchange rate of 5.50 francs to the dollar, which is probably on the low side given comparative price levels, and ignoring the EITC, which substantially increased the disposable income of low-paid American workers, we find that the US minimum wage was equivalent to F26.5 per hour net, compared with 29.7 for the French minimum wage. Of course, low-paid workers in France receive distributions in kind (health and education) not available (or less available) in the United States, but the jobless also receive those benefits, so they don't matter in regard to work incentives, which is what we are interested in here. Hence it is not certain that the attractiveness of low-wage jobs and the avoidance of poverty traps are not issues in France.

The fundamental difference, though, is obviously that the demand for labor is higher in the United States than in France. One point that is difficult to get around is that although the net minimum wages in both countries are comparable, the "super-gross" minimum wages, that is, the wages including all employer-paid charges, are quite different: US employers paid 7.5 percent in charges in 1996, for a minimum wage (from the employer's point of view) of $5.59 or F30.7 per hour, compared with charges of 44.8 percent in France in 1993, for a total of F55 an hour (reduced to F48.1 by the reduction in social charges on low-paid workers on January 1, 1997).

That is why French strategies for reducing unemployment through structural fiscal reform since the late 1970s have focused on stimulating demand for low-wage labor rather than supply: the goal is to reduce the relative cost of low-wage jobs by gradually shifting employer charges from low-wage to high-wage workers (Chapter 3). This strategy has made the schedule of charges on active workers slightly more progressive, although it remains relatively flat (Figure 4.1), and although the reductions in employer charges from 1993 to 1996 were much too concentrated on the very bottom of the wage distribution, with the attendant risk of creating "low-wage traps" (because employer costs increase very rapidly if the employer attempts to increase the worker's net wage [Piketty, 1997a]).

Regardless of whether one attempts to influence the supply of labor or the demand, what quantitative reduction of unemployment can one expect from such structural reforms? If the restructuring of employer charges is systematic and universal (rather than limited to specific categories of employers and employees), all available studies suggest that the long-term effects will be "significant." What does "significant" mean? The problem is that the elasticities of supply and demand on which these strategies are based, while not negligible, unfortunately tend to be about 1 or less, which means that the shift in taxes required to create one job is close to the market value of that job, that is, the cost to the employer per job. It is therefore tempting to conclude that the government could bear the cost itself by creating public-sector jobs, as the Scandinavian countries did to reduce unemployment in the 1980s. Or else that the government could impose job sharing by reducing working hours and compensating for the reduced purchasing power of low-paid workers. All these strategies would cost about the same in terms of francs invested per job created. Of course, one important difference is that a job in the private sector reflects consumer demand, whereas the contribution of a public-sector employee to output is sometimes more dubious. Furthermore, job creation through work sharing implicitly assumes that the currently unemployed can perform the same tasks just as well as the currently employed, which may be true in some cases but is not universally true. In any case, the effects of fiscal redistribution on unemployment have been unimpressive enough that the question is not yet settled. In addition, the private-sector jobs that one might hope to create this way, in the food service, retail, and similar sectors, are considered less valuable than the industrial jobs of the postwar boom years.

Negative Income Tax and Basic Income

A radical fiscal redistribution proposal gained a great deal of attention in the 1960s and 1970s. Milton Friedman proposed that each adult citizen should receive a certain lump sum every month, regardless of income or labor market status. The original idea was to interfere as little as possible with the virtuous mechanism of the market and to replace other forms of "social protection" with a single modest allocation (Friedman, 1962). Subsequently, Friedman's proposal was taken up by proponents of a more substantial redistribution known as "basic income" (Van Parijs, 1995). In its initial form, this universal transfer was conceived as part of a negative income tax. All existing forms of fiscal redistribution were to be replaced by taxing earned income at a single marginal rate and using the proceeds to finance the basic income transfer. The higher the desired universal transfer, the higher the marginal tax rate would have to be. George McGovern, the 1968 Democratic presidential candidate, learned this lesson to his dismay when voters realized that the flat 33.3 percent marginal rate he proposed would not be nearly enough to finance the transfer he envisaged. The basic income is thus a very different instrument from the EITC, because the latter fits into the existing fiscal redistribution system with a negative marginal rate of minus 40 percent. It does not alter existing taxes and transfers, and the additional transfer it provides is not universal but cuts off at a certain level of income.

The negative income tax and basic income proposals may at first sight seem surprising in light of the foregoing discussion. Obviously, the amount of any "universal" transfer must be smaller than the taxes levied on those earning above a certain level of income, since the transfer to those lower down the income scale has to be paid for. Why pay a basic income to everyone if it means raising taxes on a portion of the population by an amount greater than the basic income they receive? If the goal is to reduce the marginal effective rate on low-income people while preserving the same level of transfer for those who earn nothing, it would seem simpler to cut taxes (such as payroll taxes) on low earners or pay them directly while shifting the burden in the middle of the income distribution or above. Anything that the basic income can do to combat "poverty traps" can also be accomplished with existing fiscal instruments with such a universal transfer.

In fact, however, a basic income offers certain subtle advantages. It can guarantee no loss of income to welfare recipients willing to take a job, for example, and thus improve their incentive to work. If the job is subsequently lost, the worker is nevertheless guaranteed to receive at least the basic income, whereas under the existing French system, a worker who loses a job has to requalify for the RMI, with the attendant administrative delays and social stigma (Van Parijs, 1995). More generally, "left libertarians" argue that a universal transfer allows for a less inquisitorial social policy, since it is not based on the recipient's social or marital status.

Efficient Redistribution

In many situations, inequality calls for a collective effort of redistribution not only because it contradicts our sense of social justice but also because it implies a formidable waste of human resources that could be better utilized for the benefit of all. As noted previously, typical examples include discrimination and monopsony power in the labor market. It is not only insulting but also inefficient to offer fiscal compensation to the victim of unjust discrimination or exploitation by an employer. Inequality of this kind requires redistributive instruments capable not only of redistributing income but also of correcting the market failures responsible for them. Such instruments include affirmative action, minimum wage legislation, and other direct labor market interventions. Education and training policies can also serve as powerful instruments of efficient redistribution by modifying the structure of labor income inequality. We discussed these instruments in Chapter 3. Two other types of efficient redistribution have been important historically and politically: social insurance and Keynesian demand management.

Redistribution and Social Insurance

The imperfection of the credit market (or the mere fact that "people lend only to the rich") is responsible for the most transparent form of inefficient inequality. Instruments for combating it effectively have not always been easy to come by, however (see Chapter 2). In fact, the incentive and information problems that are responsible for credit rationing exist in any intertemporal market, including, in particular, the market for insurance. This may be the reason why the market has proved incapable of providing adequate social insurance, thus justifying the need for the compulsory government-provided social protection schemes that form the heart of the modern welfare state.

Efficient Social Insurance

For example, no private insurance company has ever offered a policy covering the risk of temporary unemployment and providing a suitable replacement income, despite the obvious utility of such a policy and the large number of people who would be willing to pay for one. An obvious explanation for this market failure is that it may be difficult to observe what a person actually earns, and the individual in question always has an interest in understating his income in order to pay a lower premium. The government's advantage in this respect is that, over time, it has acquired the legal and administrative capacity to monitor what employers actually pay workers and thus to establish each worker's claim to unemployment insurance.

Adverse selection is also an important factor. Companies have an interest in attracting low-risk clients, but the worker is better informed than the company about his level of risk. Companies will therefore tend to offer policies designed to separate low-risk workers from high-risk ones. Such policies will be inefficient. For instance, they may propose high deductibles or cover only minor risks. Adverse selection can be particularly problematic in the health insurance market, where individuals often have a good deal of private information about their risks. In such situations, competition may be totally inefficient, not only for high-risk individuals who may find themselves excluded from the market but also for low-risk individuals who are offered inefficient contracts. Making insurance compulsory may then be in everyone's interest even though low-risk individuals will have to subsidize high-risk ones (Rothschild and Stiglitz, 1976). The same phenomenon may also justify government regulation of other insurance markets, such as the market for automobile insurance (Henriet and Rochet, 1988).

There is also another justification for government-provided health insurance: only the seller (the health care provider) can accurately judge the cost of the service, which may lead to unjustifiably high prices and unnecessary procedures (Arrow, 1963). This argument is often used to explain why health care costs are so high in countries where private health insurance predominates, such as the United States, and to justify government regulation of health-care expenditure in public health-care systems.

The imperfection of intertemporal markets may also justify public pension systems. Adverse selection exists, since a pension is also a kind of "survival insurance." Indeed, the market for converting savings into lifetime annuities is far from perfect. Still, the problem of private information about one's own life expectancy is surely less important in regard to pensions than in regard to unemployment and health risks. The primary justification for government pensions is simply the imperfection of markets for transferring income from working years to retirement years. Low-income individuals have limited access to the kinds of investments needed to accumulate adequate retirement savings, and a state-guaranteed public pension system can compensate for this deficiency.

In these and other situations, competitive markets are often incapable of providing the goods and services that consumers value most. A compulsory public system can fill this role efficiently. It is then justifiable to treat public expenditures for these purposes separately from other government expenditures and to exclude the charges levied to finance them from the calculation of average and marginal effective rates of fiscal redistribution: if a worker goes from earning F5,000 a month to F10,000, he also doubles his claim on retirement income, and any additional charges he is required to pay for these additional rights should be counted as deferred income. If we take such deferred income into account, we have to reduce the average and marginal "effective" rates in Figure 4.1 by 15–20 points (Piketty, 1997b). A pure system, in which all social insurance would take the form of charges to purchase deferred income, would not involve redistribution at all but simply correct market imperfections in an efficient manner. Social charges would simply be payments for the coverage that individuals would desire if the market were capable of providing it.

Is Social Insurance an Instrument of Fiscal Redistribution?

Nevertheless, not all social insurance expenditures are neutral with respect to redistribution of labor income. Health insurance is the simplest case: it is financed in France by a payroll tax proportional to income, whereas most reimbursements for care, hospital fees, and the like are the same for all. Absent any efficiency justification, this redistributive effect would suffice to legitimize the system. In view of the impossibility of achieving genuine redistribution from capital to labor, compulsory public health insurance (as implemented in France) is simply a form of negative tax that provides for lump-sum transfers paid for by a proportional payroll tax. Even though this is a form of pure redistribution, there is no reason why health insurance should not be accounted separately from other forms of fiscal redistribution and paid for by a specific charge so that each individual can measure its cost relative to other expenses. Educational expenditures could be financed in a similar way.

Since there is no significant direct redistribution between active workers, as we have seen, these two forms of social expenditure, on health and education, are two main forms of contemporary redistribution. Redistribution is achieved through government spending rather than monetary transfers. Both are lump-sum transfers from which everyone benefits equally, no matter what his or her level of income (at least in regard to primary and secondary schooling), and they are financed by charges that increase proportionately or slightly progressively with income. The level of in-kind redistribution is what distinguishes countries that redistribute less from countries that redistribute more, since monetary transfers between active workers are of negligible importance everywhere. For example, a French worker paid the minimum wage is paid roughly the same amount as an American worker on minimum wage, but the American worker must pay for his own health insurance and for the education of his children, which can be quite costly. Because of this fiscal redistribution, a minimum-wage worker in France is incontestably better off than a minimum-wage worker in the United States (unless he or she is young, in good health, and childless, as minimum-wage workers often are).

The expenditures of public pay-as-you-go (PAYGO) pension systems, which account for by far the lion's share of all social spending, are quite different. The proportional payroll taxes paid during a worker's working life entitle him or her to receive transfer payments upon retirement—payments that are also proportional to past income. One might think, therefore, that the redistributive effect would be nil. In fact, inequality in retirement is primarily a matter of unequal life expectancies: broadly speaking, low-wage workers have markedly shorter life expectancies than high-income workers, so they receive pension payments for a shorter time period. The available studies that look at the French pension system in its entirety indicate that for every franc of payroll tax paid during a worker's working life, top managers receive pension payments that are more than 50 percent greater than the pension payments received by ordinary workers (Chassard and Concialdi, 1989, p. 76). In other words, pension payments redistribute upward: a substantial portion of the payroll tax paid by workers goes to finance the pensions of top managers. One must obviously bear in mind that a pension system based on private saving might leave workers without any pension at all if their savings were lost in speculation and in the imperfection of intertemporal markets. The disastrous experiences of pension funds in the interwar wars justified the establishment of PAYGO government pension plans by demonstrating the inability of the financial markets to pay defined benefits on the basis of a given savings rate. Times have changed, however: the financial products available in the 1990s offered more opportunity for collective investments with guaranteed returns, even for small savers (such as minimum-wage workers, who paid payroll taxes combining employer and employee charges of F1,500 a month in 1996).

Moving to a private pension plan would not really solve the problem of unequal life expectancies, however, because investors in these collective plans would include both high- and low earners with highly unequal life expectancies, just as the government PAYGO plans do. In any case, the main problem is obviously that the transition from one plan to another must be very gradual. It would be unjust to deprive workers near the end of their working lives of the pensions they have been promised, even if those pensions were financed in an antiredistributive manner.

Of course, public pension plans always set a floor on pensions such as *le minimum vieillesse* in France. Every retiree receives this minimum pension, even if he or she has not paid a sufficient amount in payroll taxes during working years. These pensions are certainly redistributive. What is more, it is these minimum limits on pension benefits that have made it possible to eradicate the once pervasive problem of "elder poverty" and considerably reduced household income inequality throughout the Western world. Such transfers account for only a very small portion of total pension expenses in France and elsewhere in Europe, however. Furthermore, similar minimum benefit limits exist and play the same beneficial role in countries where the public pension system was created primarily for this purpose, as in the United States and United Kingdom.

The mixed results of public pension systems also illustrate the dangers of believing the myth of "the insurance society" (Rosanvallon, 1995). If one thinks of redistribution in terms of social insurance in a society all of whose members are subject to the same "risks," against which they must be ensured collectively, one may well fail to redistribute where redistribution is needed, for example, between active workers, while establishing "redistributions" that fail to redistribute, as is the case with many pension plans and certain redistributions in kind, such as public higher education, which often become mechanisms for redistributing from low earners to high earners, as in France.

Redistribution and Demand

"Keynesian" demand management is an effective redistributive mechanism that occupies an important place in the contemporary image and practice of state intervention. In the public mind, what Keynes taught was that an increase in wages can stimulate demand for goods and services and thereby increase output and raise the level of employment. As far as redistribution is concerned, this is the best of all possible worlds, because everything improves at the same time and nobody has to pay for it. It is a powerful idea, but its conceptual and empirical foundations are relatively fragile. Why should a redistribution of demand increase the output of the economy? If it is simply a matter of transferring purchasing power from firms and capitalists to workers (which may be an excellent thing to do from the standpoint of social justice), why would overall demand increase, unless we assume that firms and capitalists are not spending their full purchasing power on either consumption or investment goods? In fact, there is little or no "dormant" purchasing power: income that is not consumed immediately is always invested somewhere in one form or another: in government bonds, for example. One possible interpretation is that if the total demand for goods and services remains constant, the composition of the consumption basket nevertheless changes, and this stimulates more output. For example, unconsumed income may not have been invested in the most useful way possible, and redistribution toward workers or mobilization of idle resources through government spending might make for a more efficient use of savings.

Another classic argument is that redistribution of purchasing power shifts demand toward goods that can be produced efficiently only on a very large scale, thus stimulating output from larger firms at the expense of smaller-scale productive units. For instance, a high level of inequality in purchasing power may prevent or delay industrialization, because the poor are too poor to generate sufficient demand for industrial goods, while the rich demand mainly imported goods and domestic services (Murphy et al., 1989; Piketty, 1994, pp. 791–794).

Clearly, then, there is no shortage of arguments to justify the idea that a redistribution of purchasing power can both diminish inequality and stimulate activity for the benefit of all. There is, however, no reason to believe that all the conditions necessary for these virtuous mechanisms to operate are satisfied simultaneously. Each case must be evaluated on its merits. Furthermore, economists nowadays usually explain Keynesian stimulus quite differently: the argument is that prices and wages do not adjust sufficiently rapidly in the short term, for example, because nominal wages are sticky, so that the only way to raise the level of employment is to lower real wages by way of inflationary stimulus. The idea that inflation can "lubricate" the gears of the economy and eliminate rigidities takes us a long way away from the best of all possible redistributive worlds, where the argument was rather that it was an increase in the purchasing power of workers that was supposed to stimulate the economy. A stimulus policy may also have other consequences, such as increasing the stock of public debt, which inevitably increases the demand for and therefore the return on capital—an unwanted redistributive effect. In any case, stimulus policies generally have short-term effects, and their long-term redistributive consequences are difficult to assess, especially when compared with the powerful structural instruments analyzed previously.

The example of Keynesian redistribution also shows how fruitless it may be always to seek an efficient redistribution that can solve every problem at once. The danger was already clear in the myth of the "insurance society," but the point is more general. For example, it is misleading and counterproductive to argue that all human capital inequality is a consequence of discrimination or that low wages are always a consequence of employer monopsony. Although it is essential to identify efficient redistribution wherever it exists, it is pointless to denounce every inequality as a sign of gross inefficiency that the right policy can eliminate. To do so is to delegitimize the taxes needed to finance fiscal transfers, which may not eliminate every imagined inequality but nevertheless help to attenuate very real inequalities in standards of living.

References

Abbreviations

AER	*American Economic Review*
JPE	*Journal of Political Economy*
QJE	*Quarterly Journal of Economics*

Adelman, I. and S. Robinson. 1989. "Income distribution and development." *Handbook of Development Economics,* vol. 2. New York: North-Holland.

Akerlof, G. and J. Yellen. 1990. "The fair wage-effort hypothesis and unemployment." *QJE* 105: 255–283.

Arrow, K. 1963. "Uncertainty and the welfare economics of medical care." *AER* 53: 941–973.

——— 1973. "The theory of discrimination." In O. Ashenfelter and A. Rees, eds., *Discrimination in Labor Markets.* Princeton: Princeton University Press.

Atkinson, A. 1983. *The Economics of Inequality.* Oxford: Clarendon Press.

Atkinson, A., L. Rainwater, and T. Smeeding. 1995. *Income Distribution in OECD Countries.* Paris: OECD.

Atkinson, A. and J. Stiglitz. 1980. *Lectures on Public Economics.* New York: McGraw-Hill.

Banerjee, A. and M. Ghatak. 1995. *Empowerment and Efficiency: The Economics of Tenancy Reform.* Cambridge, MA: MIT.

Banerjee, A. and A. Newman. 1993. "Occupational choice and the process of development." *JPE* 101: 274–299.

Becker, G. 1964. *Human Capital.* New York: Columbia University Press.

——— 1991. *A Treatise on the Family.* Cambridge, MA: Harvard University Press.

Benabou, R. 1993. "Workings of a city: Location, education, production." *QJE* 108: 619–652.

——— 1996. "Inequality and growth." NBER Working Paper 5658, in *NBER Macroeconomics Annual 1996,* vol. 11.

Bewley, T. 1994. "A field study on downward wage rigidity." New Haven: Yale University.

Blau, F. and L. Kahn. 1994. "The impact of wage structure on trends in US gender wage differentials." NBER Working Paper 4748.

Blundell, R. 1995. "The impact of taxation on labour force participation and labour supply." *OECD Jobs Study Working Papers,* 8. OECD Publishing. http://dx.doi.org/10.1787/576638686128.

Booth, A. and D. Snower. 1996. *Acquiring Skills: Market Failures, Their Symptoms and Policy Responses.* Cambridge: Cambridge University Press.

Boudon, R. 1973. *L'Inégalité des chances.* Paris: Armand Colin.

Bound, J. and R. Freeman. 1989. "Black Economic Progress: Erosion of Post-1965 Gains in the 1980s." In S. Shulman and W. Darity Jr., eds., *The Question of Discrimination: Racial Equality in the U.S. Labor Market,* pp. 32–49. Middletown, CT: Wesleyan University Press.

Bourdieu, P. and J.-C. Passeron. 1964. *Les Héritiers.* Paris: Minuit.

—— 1970. *La Reproduction.* Paris: Minuit.

Bourguignon, F. 1981. "Pareto-superiority of unegalitarian equilibria in Stiglitz' model of wealth distribution with convex savings function." *Econometrica* 49: 1469–1475.

Bourguignon, F. and M. Martinez. 1996. *Decomposition of the Change in the Distribution of Primary Family Incomes: A Microsimulation Approach Applied to France, 1979–1989.* Paris: DELTA.

Card, D. 1992. "The effect of unions on the distribution of wages: Redistribution or relabelling?" NBER Working Paper 4195.

Card, D. and R. Freeman. 1993. *Small Differences that Matter: Labor Markets and Income Maintenance in Canada and the United States.* Chicago: University of Chicago Press.

Card, D., F. Kramarz, and T. Lemieux. 1996. "Changes in the relative structure of wages and employment: A comparison of the United States, Canada and France." NBER Working Paper 5487.

Card, D. and A. Krueger. 1992. "Does school quality matter?" *JPE* 100: 1–40.

—— 1995. *Myth and Measurement: The New Economics of the Minimum Wage.* Princeton: Princeton University Press.

Chamley, C. 1996. *Capital Income Taxation, Income Distribution and Borrowing Constraints.* Paris: DELTA.

Chassard, Y. and P. Concialdi. 1989. *Les Revenus en France.* Paris: La Découverte, "Repères."

Coate, S. and G. Loury. 1993. "Will affirmative action eliminate negative stereotypes?" *AER* 83: 1220–1240.

Cohen, D., A. Lefranc, and G. Saint-Paul. 1996. "French unemployment: A transatlantic perspective." *Economic Policy* 12 (25): 265–292.

Coleman, J. 1966. *Equality of Educational Opportunity.* Washington, DC: US Dept. of Health, Education, and Welfare.

Cooper, S., S. Durlauf, and P. Johnson. 1994. "On the transmission of economic status across generations." *ASA Papers and Proceedings,* pp. 50–58.

CSERC. 1996. *Les Inégalités d'emploi et de revenu.* Paris: La Découverte.

Davis, S. 1992. "Cross-country patterns of change in relative wages." *NBER Macroeconomics Annual 1992.*

Douglas, P. 1976. "The Cobb-Douglas production function once again: Its history, its testing and some new empirical values." *JPE* 84: 903–915.

Drèze, J. and A. Sen. 1995. *India: Economic Development and Social Opportunity.* Delhi: Oxford University Press.

Ducamin, R. 1995. *Rapport de la commission d'études des prélèvements fiscaux and sociaux pesant sur les ménages.* Paris: Ministère de l'Économie et des Finances.

Duménil, G. and D. Lévy. 1996. *La Dynamique du capital: un siècle d'économie américaine.* Paris: PUF.

Ehrenberg, R. and R. Smith. 1994. *Modern Labor Economics.* New York: Harper Collins.

Eissa, N. and J. Liebman. 1996. "Labor supply response to the earned income tax credit." *QJE* 111 (2): 605–637.

Erickson, C. and A. Ichino. 1995. "Wage differentials in Italy." In R. Freeman and L. Katz, eds., *Differences and Changes in Wage Structure,* pp. 265–306. Chicago: University of Chicago Press.

Erikson, R. and J. Goldthorpe. 1992. *The Constant Flux: A Study of Class Mobility in Industrial Societies.* Oxford: Clarendon Press.

Feenberg, D. and J. Poterba. 2000. "The income and tax share of very high income households." *AER* 90 (2): 264–270.

Feldstein, M. 1995. "The effect of marginal tax rates on taxable income: A panel study of the 1986 Tax Reform Act." *JPE* 103 (3): 551–572.

Fleurbaey, M. 1996. *Théories économiques de la justice.* Paris: Economica.

Freeman, R. 1973. "Changes in the labor market status of Black Americans, 1948–1972." *Brookings Papers on Economic Activity,* no. 1, pp. 67–120.

—— 1995. "Are your wages set in Beijing?" *Journal of Economic Perspectives* 9 (3): 15–32.

—— 1996. *Disadvantaged Young Men and Crime.* Cambridge, MA: Harvard University Press.

Freeman, R. and J. Medoff. 1984. *What Do Unions Do?* New York: Basic Books.

Friedman, M. 1962. *Capitalism and Freedom.* Chicago: University of Chicago Press.

Goldin, C. and R. Margo. 1992. "The great compression: The wage structure in the United States at mid-century." *QJE* 107: 1–34.

Goolsbee, A. 1997. "What happens when you tax the rich? Evidence from executive compensation." NBER Working Paper 6333.

Gottschalk, P. 1993. "Changes in inequality of family income in seven industrialized countries." *AER* 83 (2): 136–142.

Goux, D. and E. Maurin. 1996. "Meritocracy and social heredity in France: Some aspects and trends." *European Sociological Review* 13 (2): 159–177.

Hamermesh, D. 1986. The demand for labor in the long run. In O. Ashenfelter and R. Layard, eds., *Handbook of Labor Economics,* pp. 429–471. Amsterdam: North Holland.

—— 1993. *Labor Demand.* Princeton: Princeton University Press.

Harhoff, D. and T. Kane. 1994. "Financing apprenticeship training: Evidence from Germany." NBER Working Paper 4557.

Henriet, D. and J.-C. Rochet. 1988. "Équilibres et optima sur les marchés d'assurance." In *Mélanges économiques en l'honneur d'Edmond Malinvaud.* Paris: Economica.

Herrnstein, R. and C. Murray. 1994. *The Bell Curve: Intelligence and Class Structure in American Life.* New York: The Free Press.

IMF. 1996. *World Economic Outlook.*

INSEE. 1994. "Un siècle de données macroéconomiques." *INSEE Résultats,* nos. 303–304.

—— 1995. "Revenus et patrimoine des ménages, édition 1995." *INSEE Synthèses,* no. 1.

——— 1996a. "Séries longues sur les salaires." *INSEE Résultats,* no. 457.

——— 1996b. "Revenus et patrimoine des ménages, édition 1996." *INSEE Synthèses,* no. 5.

——— 1996c. "Rapport sur les comptes de la nation 1995." *INSEE Résultats,* nos. 471, 472, 473.

——— 1996d. "L'évolution des salaires jusqu'en 1994." *INSEE Synthèses,* no. 4.

——— 2002. "Les salaires dans l'industrie, le commerce et les services en 2000." *INSEE Résultats Sociétés,* no. 7.

Judd, K. 1985. "Redistributive taxation in a simple perfect foresight model." *Journal of Public Economics* 28: 59–83.

Juhn, C., K. Murphy, and B. Pierce. 1993. "Wage inequality and the rise in returns to skill." *JPE* 101: 410–442.

Juhn, C., K. Murphy, and R. Topel. 1991. "Why has the natural rate increased over time?" *Brookings Papers on Economic Activity* 2: 75–142.

Kahneman, D., J. Knetsch and R. Thaler. 1986. "Fairness as a constraint on profit seeking." *AER* 76: 728–741.

Katz, L., G. Loveman, and D. Blanchflower. 1995. "A comparison of changes in the structure of wages in four OECD coutries." In R. Freeman and L. Katz, eds., *Differences and Changes in Wage Structure.* Chicago: University of Chicago Press.

Kolm, S. C. 1972. *Justice et équité.* Paris: Éditions du CNRS.

Kramarz, F., S. Lollivier, and L. Pelé. 1995. "Wage inequalities and firm-specific compensation policies in France." Document de travail INSEE-CREST 9518.

Kremer, M. and E. Maskin. 1996. "Wage inequality and segregation by skill." NBER Working Paper 5718.

Krueger, A. and L. Summers. 1988. "Efficiency wages and the interindustry wage structure." *Econometrica* 56: 259–293.

Krussel, P., L. Ohanian, J. V. Rios-Rull, and G. Violante. 1996. "Capital-skill complementarity and inequality." University of Rochester.

Kuznets, S. 1955. "Economic growth and economic inequality." *AER* 45: 1–28.

Landais, C. 2007. "Les hauts revenus en France (1998–2006): une explosion des inégalités?" PSE Working Paper.

Lefranc, A. 1997. "Évolutions des marchés du travail français et américains: quelques éléments d'analyse comparative." *Revue Economique* 48 (5): 1041–1060.

Lemieux, T. 1993. "Unions and wage inequality in Canada and in the United States." In D. Card and R. Freeman, eds., *Small Differences that Matter.* Chicago: University of Chicago Press.

Lhomme, J. 1968. "Le pouvoir d'achat de l'ouvrier français au cours d'un siècle: 1840–1940." *Le Mouvement social* 63: 41–70.

Liebman, J. 1996. "Essays on the earned income tax credit." PhD diss., Harvard University.

Lollivier, S. and D. Verger. 1996. "Patrimoine des ménages: déterminants et disparités." *Économie et Statistique* 296–297: 13–32.

Lucas, R. 1990a. "Supply-side economics: An analytical review." Oxford Economic Papers 42, pp. 293–316.

———— 1990b. "Why doesn't capital flow from rich to poor countries?" *AER* 80: 92–96.

Mankiw, G., D. Romer, and D. Weil. 1992. "A contribution to the empirics of economic growth." *QJE* 107: 407–437.

Meyer, C. 1995. "Income distribution and family structure." PhD diss., MIT.

Morrisson, C. 1991. "L'inégalité des revenus." In M. Lévy-Leboyer and J.-C. Casanova, eds., *Entre l'État et le marché: l'économie française de 1880 à nos jours.* Paris: Gallimard.

———— 1996. *La Répartition des revenus.* Paris: PUF.

Mulligan, C. 1996. *Parental Priorities and Economic Inequality.* Chicago: University of Chicago Press.

Murphy, K., A. Shleifer, and R. Vishny. 1989. "Income distribution, market size and industrialization." *QJE* 104: 537–564.

Murphy, K. and F. Welch. 1993a. "Inequality and relative wages." *AER* 83 (2): 104–109.

———— 1993b. "Occupational change and the demand for skill." *AER* 83 (2): 122–126.

Neumark, D. and W. Wascher. 1994. "Employment effects of minimum and subminimum wages: Reply to Card, Katz and Krueger." *Industrial and Labor Relations Review* 48: 497–512.

Nizet, J.-Y. 1990. *Fiscalité, économie et politique: l'impôt en France, 1945–1990.* Paris: LGDJ.

OECD. 1985. *The Integration of Women in the Economy.* Paris: OECD.

—— 1993. *Perspectives de l'emploi,* July. Paris: OECD.

—— 1995. *Statistiques des recettes publiques des pays membres de l'OCDE, 1965–1994.* Paris: OECD.

—— 1996. Economic Outlook no. 59, June. Annual Projections for OECD Countries. http://stats.oecd.org/ Paris: OECD.

—— 2000. *Taux de chômage standardisés* (www.oecd.org). Paris: OECD.

Phelps, E. 1968. "The statistical theory of racism and sexism." *AER* 62: 659–661.

—— 1994. *Structural Slumps: The Modern Equilibrium Theory of Unemployment, Interest and Assets.* Cambridge, MA: Harvard University Press.

Piketty, T. 1994. "Inégalités et redistribution." *Revue d'économie politique* 104: 769–800.

—— 1995. "Social mobility and redistributive politics." *QJE* 110: 551–584.

—— 1997a. "La redistribution fiscale face au chômage." *Revue française d'économie.*

—— 1997b. "Les créations d'emploi en France et aux États-Unis: 'services de proximité' contre 'petits boulots?'" *Notes de la fondation Saint-Simon* 93 (December). See also *Économie et Statistique* 318 (1998–8): 73–99.

—— 1998. "L'impact des incitations financières au travail sur les comportements individuels: une estimation pour le cas français." *Économie et Prévision* 132–133 (Jan.-Mar.): 1–35.

—— 1999. "Les hauts revenus face aux modifications des taux marginaux supérieurs de l'impôt sur le revenu en France, 1970–1996." *Économie et Prévision* 138–139 (Apr.-Sept.): 25–60.

—— 2001. *Les Hauts Revenus en France au XXe siècle. Inégalités et redistributions 1901–1998.* Paris: Grasset.

Piketty, T. and E. Saez. 2003. "Income inequality in the United States, 1913–1998." *QJE* 118: 1–39.

Rawls, J. 1972. *A Theory of Justice.* Oxford: Clarendon Press.

Roemer, J. 1996. *Theories of Distributive Justice.* Cambridge, MA: Harvard University Press.

Rosanvallon, P. 1995. *La Nouvelle Question sociale.* Paris: Seuil.

Rothemberg, J. 1996. "Ideology and the distribution of income." Cambridge, MA: MIT.

Rothschild, M. and J. Stiglitz. 1976. "Equilibrium in competitive insurance markets." *QJE* 90: 629–650.

Shavit, Y. and H. P. Blossfeld. 1993. *Persistent Inequality: Changing Educational Attainment in 13 Countries.* Boulder: Westview.

Slemrod, J. 1995. "Income creation or income shifting? Behavioral responses to the *Tax Reform Act* of 1986." *AER* 85 (2): 175–180.

Solow, R. 1956. "A contribution to the theory of economic growth." *QJE* 70: 65–94.

—— 1958. "A skeptical note on the constancy of relative shares." *AER* 48: 618–631.

Spence, M. 1974. *Market Signalling: Informational Transfer in Hiring and Related Screening Processes.* Cambridge, MA: Harvard University Press.

Topel, R. 1993. "What have we learned from empirical studies of unemployment and turnover?" *AER* 83: 110–115.

Van Parijs, P. 1995. *Real Freedom for All: What (If Anything) Can Justify Capitalism?* Oxford: Clarendon Press.

Williamson, J. 1985. *Did British Capitalism Breed Inequality?* Boston: Allen & Unwin.

Williamson, J. and P. Lindert. 1980. *American Inequality: A Macroeconomic History.* New York: Academic Press.

Wilson, W. J. 1987. *The Truly Disadvantaged: The Inner City, the Underclass and Public Policy.* Chicago: University of Chicago Press.

Wolff, E. 1992. "Changing inequality of wealth." *AER* 82 (2): 552–558.

Young, A. 1995. "The tyranny of numbers: Confronting the statistical realities of the East Asian growth miracles." *QJE* 110: 641–680.

Contents in Detail

Note to the Reader · vii

Introduction · 1

1. The Measurement of Inequality and Its Evolution · 5
  Different Types of Income · 5
  Wage Inequality · 8
    International Comparisons · 10
  Income Inequality · 12
    International Comparisons · 14
  Inequalities in Time and Space · 16
  The Historical Evolution of Inequality · 17
    From Laws of History to Uncertainties · 20
    From Wages to Incomes · 22
    Inequality with Respect to Employment · 23

2. Capital-Labor Inequality · 26
  The Share of Capital in Total Income · 27
    The Question of Capital/Labor Substitution · 27
      What Capital/Labor Substitution Means · 29
      Redistribution: "Fiscal" or "Direct"? · 30
      The Elasticity of Substitution between Capital and Labor · 32
      The Elasticity of Capital Supply · 35
      Are Capitalists and the Price System Necessary? · 37
    A Compromise between Short-Term and Long-Term Theories? · 40
      From Share of Value-Added to Household Income · 41
      What the Constancy of the Profit Share Tells Us · 45
      Who Pays Social Charges (Payroll Taxes)? · 46
      A Cobb-Douglas Production Function? · 48
      Historical Time versus Political Time? · 49
      Why Has the Profit Share Not Increased in the United States
        and United Kingdom? · 53

The Dynamics of the Distribution of Capital · 55
 The Theory of Perfect Credit and Convergence · 56
  The Question of Convergence between Rich and
   Poor Countries · 57
 The Problem of Capital Market Imperfections · 60
  Possible Public Interventions · 62
  A Flat Tax on Capital? · 64

3. Inequality of Labor Income · 66
 Inequality of Wages and Human Capital · 66
  The Explanatory Power of the Theory of Human Capital · 68
   Important Historical Inequalities · 68
   Supply and Demand · 69
   The Rise of Wage Inequality since 1970 · 70
   Skill-Biased Technological Change? · 71
   Wage Inequality and Globalization · 73
  How to Redistribute Labor Income · 74
   A Major Political Issue · 76
  Where Does Human Capital Inequality Come From? · 78
   Efficient Inequality? · 79
   The Role of the Family and Educational Expenses · 81
   The Problem of Inefficient Segregation of Human Capital · 83
   Discrimination in the Labor Market · 85
   Affirmative Action versus Fiscal Transfers · 86
 The Social Determination of Wage Inequality · 88
  The Role of Unions in Setting Wages · 89
   Unions as Substitutes for Fiscal Redistribution? · 90
   Do Unions Contribute to Economic Efficiency? · 92
  The Monopsony Power of Employers · 94
   When Does a Higher Minimum Wage Increase the Level
    of Employment? · 95
  Efficiency Wages and Fair Wages · 97
   National Traditions and Wage Inequality · 98

4. Instruments of Redistribution · 100

Pure Redistribution · 100

Average and Marginal Rates of Redistribution · 100

The Absence of Redistribution between Workers · 102

The U-Shaped Curve of Marginal Rates · 104

Just Fiscal Redistribution · 105

Do High Taxes Diminish Revenue? · 106

The Earned Income Tax Credit in the United States · 108

Fiscal Redistribution to Reduce Unemployment? · 109

Negative Income Tax and Basic Income · 112

Efficient Redistribution · 113

Redistribution and Social Insurance · 114

Efficient Social Insurance · 114

Is Social Insurance an Instrument of Fiscal Redistribution? · 116

Redistribution and Demand · 119

Index

Adoption studies, education outcomes
 and, 82
Adverse selection: credit markets
 and, 60–61; pension systems and,
 115–116; social insurance and, 115
Affirmative action, 86–88, 114
Africa: income inequality, 15; rates of
 growth, 58
African Americans, discrimination
 against, 85–88
Aggregate production function, of
 Solow, 30
Agriculture, direct redistribution of
 capital and, 63–64
Allocative role, of price system, 30–33,
 37–40, 100
Arrow, Kenneth, 85
Asia: growth rate per capita, 58, 59;
 income inequality, 15; savings
 rates, 57
Average and marginal rates of
 redistribution, 100–102, 102f;
 absence of redistribution between
 workers, 102–104; compulsory
 public systems and, 116; Earned
 Income Tax Credit in US and,
 108–109; negative income tax
 and basic income, 112–113; social
 justice and, 105–106; taxes and
 revenue, 106–108; unemployment and, 109–112; U-shaped
 curve of marginal rates, 104–105,
 109

Basic income, guaranteed, 3, 23, 104,
 112–113
Becker, Gary, 67, 78, 81

Behavioral differences, wealth
 inequality and, 13
Belgium, 14
Bell Curve, The (Herrnstein and
 Murray), 82
Bernstein, Eduard, 18
Binding wage schedules, 92–93
Busing, school integration and human
 capital, 84

Cambridge capital controversy,
 30, 39
Canada, and income inequality, 10,
 14, 23
Capital: flat tax on, 64–65; unequal
 ownership of, 26. See also Distribution of capital
Capital income: income inequality
 and, 12, 13; share received by
 households, 5–8, 6t, 44–45; social
 charges and, 34, 46–48; source of,
 42–43; taxation of, 36–37, 43,
 64–65. See also Income, share of
 capital in
Capitalism: capital-labor substitution, 39; Cobb-Douglas production function, 48; critics of and
 credit rationing, 61–62, 64;
 increases in inequality and,
 17–18, 98
Capital-labor inequality, 26–27;
 capital-labor substitution, 27–40;
 classic and marginalist theories,
 40–55; dynamics of distribution of
 capital, 55–65
Capital-labor substitution, 27–30;
 elasticity of, 32–35, 37–39, 48–49,

Capital-labor substitution *(continued)*
51–54, 75–76; elasticity of capital
supply, 35–37, 39; fiscal and direct
redistribution, 30–32; market
economy and price system, 37–40
Card, David, 95–96
Classical and marginalist theories, of
capital-labor split, 29–30, 39–40,
41*t;* Cobb-Douglas production
function and, 48–49; economic
value added and, 42–43; household
income distribution, 41, 44–45;
political and historical time and,
41*t,* 49–53, 50*t;* profit share
constancy and, 41*t,* 45–46; profit
share in United Kingdom and
United States, 41*t,* 53–55; share of
social charges, 46–48
Clinton, Bill, 96
Cobb-Douglas production function,
33–34, 48–49
Coleman, James, and report by, 82,
83–84
Collectivization, of means of
production, 39, 62, 63–64
Competition: credit markets and, 57,
61; social insurance and, 115; taxes
and, 37, 65
Compulsory education, human capital
and, 80–81
Conditional convergence, 59
Convergence, between rich and poor
countries, 57–60
C ratios, labor inequality and,
76–77
Credit markets: convergence between
rich and poor countries, 57–60;
imperfection of, 58–65, 69, 80–81,
114; perfect credit market theory
and, 56–57, 78
Credit rationing, 61–62, 64

Deferred income, social insurance and,
116
Demand management, redistribution
and, 114, 119–121
Denmark: social protection, 47–48;
wage inequality, 10
Development banks, as possible
intervention in credit market, 62–63
Direct redistribution: agriculture and,
63–64; elasticity of substitution
between capital and labor, 30–35,
48–49; fiscal redistribution and, 28,
31, 98; inequality of labor income
and, 75–76; unions and, 90–91
Disadvantaged communities, human
capital and, 82–83
Discrimination, in labor market,
85–88, 113–114, 121
Distribution of capital, dynamics of,
55–56; capital market imperfections, 60–65; perfect credit and
convergence, 56–60
D ratios: sources of household income,
6*t;* wage inequality, 8–10, 9*t*

Earned Income Tax Credit (EITC), in
US, 108–109, 112
Economic efficiency: distribution of
capital, 55, 57, 61, 65; human capital,
86; unions and, 92–94
Economic value added: capital income
and labor income, 41*t,* 42; capital
share of (1979–1995), 50*t;* complica-
tions of calculating, 43
Education: human capital and, 67,
69–70, 79–84, 92–93; redistribution
and, 59–60, 117; wage inequality
and, 72–73, 99
Efficiency wages, 97–99
Efficient redistribution, 35, 62–63, 67,
113–114; demand management and,

119–121; egalitarian education policy and, 59, 80; minimum wage and, 94–95; Pareto efficiency and, 2–3, 79; social insurance, 114–119. *See also Human capital entries*

Elasticity of substitution between capital and labor, 32–35, 37–39, 48–49, 51–54, 75–76

Elasticity of supply of capital, 35–37, 39

Elasticity of supply of human capital, 78–79, 82–83, 87, 107

Employment: inequality with respect to, 23–25; job creation and elasticity of substitution between capital and labor, 51, 53–55. *See also* Unemployment

Estate tax, progressive, 19, 64

Failure, human capital and self-fulfilling prophecies, 84–85

Fair wages, 97–99

Family, human capital and role of, 81–83

Family quotient system, in France, 87–88, 103, 107–108

Fiscal incidence, of taxes and social charges, 32, 46–48, 52

Fiscal redistribution: direct redistribution and, 28, 31, 98; and elasticity of substitution between capital and labor, 30–35, 48–49; inequality of labor income and, 75–76; unions as substitutes for, 90–92. *See also* Taxes

Flat tax, on capital, 64–65

France: attitudes toward inequality, 99; average and marginal rates of redistribution, 102, 102*f;* capital and labor shares of value added, 41*t;* effective minimum wage, 110–111; Generalized Social Contribution, 34,

38; household income sources, 6*t;* income inequality, 12–15, 12*t,* 24–25; income inequality (1870–1994), 16–17, 16*t;* income inequality, historical evolution of, 18–19, 22; minimum wage, 91; percentage of obligatory taxes, 101; profit share in, 49–55, 50*t;* social charges, 46–48; taxes receipts as percent of GDP, 44; unions in, 91–92; wage inequality, 8–11, 11*t,* 72–73

Freeman, Richard, 87–88

Friedman, Milton, 1, 3, 112

Generalized Social Contribution (CSG), in France, 34, 38

Geographic mobility, wage inequality and human capital, 96

Germany: employment, 24, 25; income inequality, 14; percentage of obligatory taxes, 101; profit share, 53; unions, 91–92; wage inequality, 10, 91, 99

Gini coefficient, 10

Globalization: market integration, 59–60; wage inequality, 73–74

Goolsbee, Austen, 107

Grameen Bank, 63

Grenelle Accords (1968), 49

Gross operating surplus (GOS), 42

Guaranteed basic income, 3, 23, 104, 112–113

Hamermesh, Daniel, 49

Health insurance: adverse selection and, 115; justifications for compulsory, 115–117; as percentage of social charges in 1966 France, 103

Herrnstein, Richard, 82, 87

Hidden underemployment, 25

Household size, income and, 12, 14, 22

Human capital: elasticity of supply of, 78–79, 82–83, 87, 107; measuring types of productivity and, 98; unequal distribution of, 58–60; wage inequality and, 88–89, 92–99

Human capital, structural causes of inequality, 78–79; affirmative action versus fiscal transfers, 86–88; discrimination in labor market and, 85–86; efficiency and, 79–81; inefficient social integration and, 83–84; role of family and education expenses, 81–83

Human capital theory, 66–68; globalization and wage inequality, 73–74; historical inequalities and, 68–69; rise of wage inequality since 1970, 70–71; skill-biased technological change and, 71–73, 76–77, 92; supply and demand and, 69–70

Incentives: basic income and, 113; credit markets and, 60, 62, 114; effects of redistribution on, 105–110; of households to save and invest, 35; human capital and investments, 78–88, 90, 93; of owners to accumulate capital and invest, 28–29

Income: distribution by deciles and centiles, 5–8, 6t; household size and, 12; inequality of, 12–16, 12t, 15t; inequality of, historical evolution, 17–25, 19f, 21t; left-right debate about inequality of, 1–3; types and distribution of, 5–8, 6t. See also Capital income; Wage entries

Income, share of capital in: capital-labor substitution, 27–40; classic and marginalist theories, 40–55. See also Capital income

Income tax, progressive, 19, 48, 64, 102–103, 106

India: human capital, 59–60, 80, 85; inequality, 16, 17

Individual self-interest, economic organization and, 39, 106

Inflation, as stimulus, 121

Information: credit markets and problems of, 61; insurance markets and, 114–115; prices and, 38

Inheritance of capital, 26; progressive tax on estates, 19, 64

Insurance society, myth of, 119, 121

Integration of schools, human capital and, 84

Intergenerational mobility, human capital and, 81, 83

Intermediate consumption, as share of firms' costs, 42

Intertemporal markets, 60–61, 114, 115–116, 118

Italy: historical evolution of inequality, 21; labor participation rate, 25; profit share, 53; unemployment, 24

Katz, Larry, 96

Keynes, John Maynard, 40; demand management, 114, 119–121

Kolm, Serge-Christophe, 2

Krueger, Alan, 95–96

Kuznets curve, 18–20, 22, 66

Kuznets, Simon, 18

Labor income: as share of firms' costs, 42; ways of redistributing, 74–77. See also Elasticity of substitution between capital and labor; Wage entries

Labor market participation rate, 25, 108

Left-right conflict, about inequality and redistribution, 1–3

Lollivier, Stéfan, 13
Lucas, Robert, 59
Luxembourg Income Study (LIS),
14, 22

Marginalist theory, of capital-labor
split. *See* Classical and marginalist
theories, of capital-labor split
Marginal productivity of labor,
capital-labor substitution and,
29–30, 34, 59
Marginal rates of redistribution.
See Average and marginal rates of
redistribution
Market economy. *See* Price system
Marx, Karl, 26, 30, 39; proletarianization thesis of, 17–18
Maximin principle, of Rawls, 2, 35,
106
McGovern, George, 112
Means of production, collectivizing of,
39, 62, 63–64
Minimum wage: EITC and, 109;
health insurance and, 103; monopsony power of employers, 96; raising
of, and effect on level of employment, 95–96; redistribution and,
75, 94; unions and, 91; in US and
France, 50, 110–111, 117; wage
distribution and, 8
Monopoly power, of unions, 89, 94
Monopsony power, of employers,
94–96, 113–114, 121
Moral hazard, credit markets and,
60–61
Murray, Charles, 82, 87

Negative income tax, 1, 3, 112–113
Nonwage compensation, 6*t*, 8, 12, 13.
See also Self-employment
compensation

Norway: historical evolution of
inequality, 22; income inequality,
14; wage inequality, 10

OECD countries: evolution of shares
of profits and wages, 49–53, 50*t*;
historical evolution of inequality,
21; income inequality, 14–15, 15*t*;
wage inequality, 10–11, 11*t*

Panel Study of Income Dynamics
(PSID), 83
Pareto efficiency, 2–3, 57, 79
Part-time work, income inequality
and, 25
Pay-as-you-go (PAYGO) pension
systems, 117–118
Payroll taxes. *See* Social charges
Pension plans: private, 118; public,
115–119
Phelps, Edmund, 85
Poverty traps, human capital and, 108,
110, 113
P ratios: income inequality, 12–14, 12*t*,
15*t*, 16–17, 23–25, 76–77; inequality's historical evolution, 20–23,
21*t*; minimum wage, 91; P defined,
7; sources of household income
and, 6*t*; wage inequality, 8–11, 77
Price system: allocative role of, 30–33,
37–40, 100; elasticity of substitution and, 32–40; housing and
educational outcomes, 84; role
in capital-labor share of total
income, 27–30, 32; social justice
and, 106
Primary distribution, 28
Prison population, underemployment
and, 24
Private sector jobs, unemployment and
fiscal redistribution, 111–112

Profit share: constancy of, 41*t*, 45–46; historical and political time and, 49–53; in US and UK, 53–55

Progressive estate tax, 19, 64

Progressive income tax, 19, 48, 64, 102–103, 106

Public investment banks, as possible intervention in credit market, 62–63

Public-sector jobs: pensions and, 115–119; unemployment and fiscal redistribution, 111–112; wages, 10

Purchasing power, of workers: changes in twentieth century, 45, 50–51, 68–69, 91, 96, 111; inequality in time and space, 16–17, 16*t*; redistribution of, 120–121

Pure redistribution, 32, 55, 67; absence of redistribution between workers, 102–104; average and marginal rates of redistribution, 100–102, 102*f*; Earned Income Tax Credit, in US, 108–109; fiscal redistribution to reduce unemployment and, 109–112; fundamental purposes of, 105–106; high taxes and revenue, 106–108; negative income tax and basic income, 112–113; Pareto efficiency and, 2–3; U-shaped curve of marginal rates, 104–105, 109

Rawls, John, 2, 35, 106

Redistributive policy, left-right conflict about, 1–3. *See also* Average and marginal rates of redistribution; Direct redistribution; Efficient redistribution; Fiscal redistribution

Rentier society, 19–20, 19*f*

Retained earnings, elasticity of capital supply and, 36–37

Retirees: income distribution and, 5, 6*t*, 7; social charges and, 101. *See also* Pension plans

Ricardo, David, 30

RMI, in France, 113

Rothenberg, Jerome, 98

Savings: behavioral differences and, 13; credit markets and, 56–57, 60; elasticity of capital supply and, 35–37; Marx and, 39; pensions and, 115–116, 118

Self-employment: calculation of value added, 43; compensation as percentage of household income, 5, 6*t*; credit rationing and, 62; income inequality and, 12

Self-interest, and economic organization, 39, 106

Singapore, 58

Skill-biased technological change, 71–73, 76–77, 92

Social charges: average and marginal rates of redistribution, 100–102, 108; employer-employee shares of, 46–48, 104–105; fiscal incidence and, 52–53; as political issue, 76–77; price of labor and, 32, 42–44; shifting burden of from low- to high-wage jobs, 34, 76–77, 111, 113, 119; unemployment and, 110–111

Social income: household income and, 5, 6*t*, 7, 105; income inequality and, 12, 23; taxes and, 47

Social insurance: efficient redistribution and, 114–116; as instrument of fiscal redistribution, 116–119; markets as intertemporal markets, 61

Social integration, housing and educational outcomes and human capital, 83–84

Social justice: left-right consensus about fundamental principles of, 1–2; left's skepticism about taxes and, 38, 52, 76; methods of redistribution and economic efficiency, 2–3, 32, 35–37, 55–57, 61, 64–65, 74, 105–106

Social origin, influence on human capital, 80–81

Solow, Robert, 30, 48, 59

South America: growth rate per capita, 58; human capital, 59; income inequality, 15

South Korea, 58

Stimulus programs, redistribution and, 121

Subsidized loans, as possible intervention in credit market, 62–63

Supply and demand: human capital and wages, 68, 69–70, 73–74, 88–89; unemployment and social charges, 111–112. *See also* Demand management

Sweden: historical evolution of inequality, 22; income inequality, 14; percentage of obligatory taxes in, 101; wage inequality, 10

Taiwan, 58

Taxes: average and marginal rates of redistribution, 100–105; capital income and, 28–32, 36–37, 43–44, 64–65; Earned Income Tax Credit, in US, 108–109, 112; effect on disposable income, 14, 22–23; Left's skepticism of redistribution through, 38, 52, 76; negative income tax, 1, 3, 112–113; progressive, on

estates, 19, 64; progressive, on income, 19, 48, 64, 102–103, 106; receipts as percent of GDP, 44; redistribution methods, 31–35, 75–76; revenue and, 106–108. *See also* Social charges

Theil and Atkinson indices, 10

Time and space, income inequality and, 16–17, 16*t*

Underemployment, 24–25, 71–72

Unemployment: efficiency wages and, 97–98; elasticity of substitution between capital and labor, 34; fiscal redistribution and, 94–95, 109–112; inequality with respect to, 13, 23–25; skill-biased technological change and, 71–72; unemployment insurance, 100, 104, 114–115; unions and, 90; U-shaped curve of marginal rates, 104–105

Unions: capital-labor split and, 28, 52; economic efficiency and, 92–94; monopoly power of, 94, 97; role in setting wages, 88–90; as substitutes for fiscal redistribution, 90–92; tax reforms of 1980s and 1990s and, 38

United Kingdom: capital and labor shares of value added, 41*t*; changes in wages, 69; constancy of profit share, 41*t*, 53–55; faith in capitalism, 98; income inequality and, 14, 18, 20–25; percentage of obligatory taxes in, 101; power of unions, 91; social charges, 46–48; wage inequality, 10, 74, 77

United States: capital and labor shares of value added, 41*t*; changes in wages, 70; constancy of profit share, 41*t*, 53–55; effective minimum wage, 110–111; EITC in, 108–110;

United States *(continued)*
faith in capitalism, 98; income inequality and, 14, 15, 18, 22–25; marginal income tax rate, 106, 107; percentage of obligatory taxes, 101; power of unions, 91; prison population, 24; social charges, 46–48; wage inequality, 10, 11, 72–73, 74
U-shaped curve of marginal rates, 104–105, 109

Value-added tax (VAT), 44–45, 103. *See also* Economic value added
Verger, Daniel, 13

Wage inequality, 8–11, 9*t,* 11*t;* historical evolution of, 20–21; human capital and, 66–74; human capital and, structural causes of, 78–88;

unemployment and underemployment, 23–25; in US and UK, 53
Wage inequality, social determination of, 88–89; efficiency wages and fair wages, 97–98; monopsony power of employers, 94–96; national traditions and, 98–99; role of unions in setting wages, 89–94
Wages: binding wage schedules, 92–93; capital-labor substitution and, 30–32; labor income and capital share, 42; as percentage of household income, 5–7, 6*t. See also Wage inequality entries*
Welfare state: basic income and, 113; EITC and, 108–109; limits of, 108; redistribution and intent of, 47, 105, 114. *See also* Social charges
Women, labor market improvements and, 87–88